WORSHIP IS...

BY STACEY HILLIAR

Stacey has a way of unpacking the jewels of the Gospel in ways that are not only enlightening, but easy to understand. In her book *Worship Is*, she does this brilliantly using personal stories, Scripture and insights in a light-hearted, easy to digest format. But don't be fooled—these thoughts are deeply profound and will weave a rich tapestry into the thread of your own personal worship life. This is not just a book for musicians, singers and worship leaders. It's a book for everyone who desires to worship God in Spirit and in truth. If you have not understood what true worship is, or you simply want to go deeper in your adoration of the Father, I highly recommend this book. Stacey carries an authentic and anointed voice for this hour. She doesn't just preach it, she doesn't just sing it, she is someone who breathes worship and lives in adoration of our amazing God daily.

Roma Waterman

Award winning songwriter/author, worship leader, speaker
Founder of HeartSong Creative Academy

Stacey Hilliar is not only a world-class person, she is a lightning rod for the Kingdom of God. She is a conduit of God's presence that translates God's heart and mind and directs it to bless the lives of everyone around her. Her life has blessed a countless number of people and pointed them in worship to the lover of her soul, Jesus. Her book *Worship Is* is a must read for every person who is curious about what living a life of worship actually means. Stacey is a brilliant communicator who has taken one of life's BIG ideas and made it accessible to everyone, even over a cup of coffee. Christians, churches and worship teams will be much better off for reading this book. I consider it a privilege to lead alongside her and even better yet, to call her a friend.

Corey Turner
Author, Prophet and Global Apostolic Leader, Neuma Church

This book is an extraordinary gift to anyone who seeks to live a life of worship in close proximity to the heart of God. It is biblical, personal, honest and insightful. Stacey devotes her life to the One she worships and through the gift of her words, has a way of awakening in others what it looks like to live a life surrendered to God. She is a visionary leader, prophet and worshipper. *Worship Is* will help you, teach you and inspire you.

Simone Turner
Author, Global Apostolic Leader, Neuma Church

Every believer should read *Worship Is* and it ought to be essential reading for all worship leaders. Stacey Hilliar has provided valuable insights into worshiping and relating to God from a treasure chest of biblical material as well as her own life experience; as a daughter of God, a worshiper, a prophet and leader in the church. Read it. Meditate on it. Digest it. It will change your view of God and how you worship!

Dr Michael Grechko
Dip.Min., B.Th., D.Min, Global Teaching Executive of Neuma Church, Principal of Neuma College

CONTENTS

ACKNOWLEDGEMENTS

Father God—thank you for choosing me. Thank you for loving me. Thank you for dreaming me. Thank you for making me your little Freedom Fighter. Jesus—you are the prize. You are the reward. Thank you for saving me. Thank you for taking my place. Thank you for bearing the weight. Thank you for calling me 'friend'. I want to live like you. I want to love like you. I want to worship like you. I will never tire of meeting you in our secret place. Holy Spirit—thank you for teaching me. Thank you for comforting me. Thank you for leading me in worship. I will spend my life chasing the wind and I will love every moment.

Jai—my one and only. You love me completely and patiently. You make me feel safe. You nudge me when I get stuck. You breathe on my dreams and tell me I can when I don't believe it. You are the only one who sees how deeply I 'feel' things and you never resent that about me. Instead, you gently lead us in prayer. You love all of me and never ask me to be smaller because you know who you are. I have loved growing up with you and am forever grateful that we will grow old together. I love our life together and I'm so grateful that you'll forever keep my toes warm.

To my children: Hope Freedom—loved but never held on earth. You now sing and dance free in the atmosphere of Heaven that your mama spends her life chasing. I can't wait to hold you and hear your song in person, my girl. Until then, sing and dance while you wait. I'll meet you in the garden.

Noah Israel—you are strong, kind and sensitive. You make people feel safe. You are consistent and you are wise. You healed me in so many ways. I am proud of you, my son, and love watching you discover your place in God's Kingdom. You are an advocate for the lonely and your sense of righteousness, grounded in love, is a gift from God and a gift to the world. Spread your wings.

Elisha Jai—you and your sister wrote eternity on my heart. You gave me the gift of understanding that I live in the in-between. One day, I will hold you and smell your sunshine smell and we will no longer feel the pain of separation. Your mama knows you war with me when I fight with a melody. I love you, Son.

Cabe Zion—you are a weapon for the Kingdom. You have made hell shudder from the womb. You are stronger than you know. Your prophetic words and prayers over my life have shaped decisions and choices, and set me on the right path. Your words are like swords, and together, as we learn how to wield that sword, you will keep me laughing endlessly. You have been forged in fire and come out not smelling of smoke. Start where I finish, Son. Write what I don't get to write. Sing what I don't get to sing. Preach what I don't get to preach.

River McKenzie—your strength is your humility and gentleness. You are so loving, thoughtful and kind. You have been given a mind that is truly remarkable. I can't wait to see people understand God and His Word through your mind and your revelation. When no one else has noticed that I am feeling a little sad or down, you have sidled up to me and offered your tiny shoulder and your loving arms. You minister love and bring life and healing to everyone and everything—you were named to do this. I'm so proud of you.

Eden Isabel—my living, breathing reminder of my Eden-like state. My mini-me. You are God's special gift straight from His heart to mine. You take my breath away. You are pure and you are our delight. You are a thousand answered prayers and a million dreams all rolled into one little human being. You are my sunshine forever. You light up a room. I am so proud of you, my girl.

Mum and Dad—thank you for teaching me how to love God, to love His Word, and to love His Church. I am grateful for you and my siblings—Hagar, Damien, Asten and Tenielle! To my in-laws (McKenzie and Hilliar) and my nieces and nephews. I'm so grateful for each one of you. People say that you can't choose your family. I'd choose you lot any day.

Ps Corey and Simone—thank you for being my pastors and friends. Thank you for believing in me, and many others, and for encouraging us to dream bigger and to believe for more. Thank you for being a safe place. Thank you for loving the Holy Spirit and for always being willing to risk it for the supernatural biscuit. Our families just fit, and I'm so grateful to God. I honour you and love you. Building the Kingdom with you is a reward. Love you Chels, Zack and Josh. (I'm not mentioning Maverick.)

To the many leaders who have shaped my life and continue to do so—I thank you and I honour you. Firstly, to my parents, Rob and Jenny McKenzie; to Ps Philip and Barbara Hills, Ps Bruce and Fiona Hills and Ps David and Sally Doery. Each of you have invested in me and believed in me. I am so grateful for your lives and your wisdom.

To Roma Waterman (Ted, Angel and Asa), for befriending me and cheering me on with a security that is rare and beautiful. You are my long-lost sister. You are a pioneer in prophetic worship. I honour you. We are the Hendos.

To my fellow Neuma Executives—Rob and Carol, Raef and Nermeen, Joseph and Blessy, Erin, Sharee, and Dr Mike and Sue. We are pioneering the seven-pillar, five-fold together, and it's an honour to break ground with you.

My rocks(tars)—Kai and Sue Mei, Joel and Bek, Marie and Brenno, and Sammy—you have protected me, guarded me, dreamt with me, laughed and cried with me, spoken truth to me. You are woven throughout the pages of this book because you are woven into my heart and life. There is deep contentment in seeing you forge a path beyond my wildest dreams and watching you start where I finish. I am a rich woman to know you and to love you. We go to war together week in and week out, and I know that we have each other's back, and together, our eyes are always on the prize. We're not afraid to get there, bloody and dirty, as long as we're doing it together. We also sit in His presence together and talk endlessly about the Bible, our dreams and worship. We do the ebb and flow of music and life together. You are part of my symphony, and it's beautiful.

To the team who have made this book happen—Rachael Tan. Thank you for hearing my heart through bad grammar and attempted gangsta jokes. You're very gifted at what you do, and your heart for worship has helped bring this to life. To my designer, Sheron—you put colour and font to the vision in my heart. Thank you for keeping things simple and uncomplicated. You are beautiful inside and out. Anton Bekker—thanks for telling me to just get on with it and to stop talking about it. You're the real deal. You lit a spark in me and I'm forever grateful for my time on the coast with you, Bev and that crazy Italian lady. And thank you Megs. For always having my back and being equally as excited about my dreams as you are about your own.

My Neuma worship family—you are a magnificent example of the Body of Christ working as it is meant to, with each person playing their part. You love the Bride, and putting a song in her mouth and a melody to her confession. You have loved me, stretched me, taught me and supported me. You have been patient with me when I've made mistakes. It is my honour to love and serve you.

My Neuma Church family—your combined love song to Jesus is my favourite sound on earth. Thank you for letting me into your hearts and lives. Thank you for allowing me to make mistakes, to grow, to try new things and to be myself. Your trust in worship is a gift that I do not take for granted. I love you individually, and I love what you represent—the Body of Christ and

Jesus' Bride. We have been placed together by God, and together, we are a glimpse of Heaven on earth—every tribe, tongue, culture, age and walk of life—united in love for our Jesus. Here at Neuma, we share in a spiritual heritage that is revival. We stand on the soil of ancient wells of revival that were birthed in prayer and bathed in worship. Let's make that our legacy together... the sound and testimony of revival... birthed in prayer and bathed in worship.

INTRODUCTION
'Caption This'

One of my favourite things to do is play the social media game, 'caption this'. I have really funny friends, so it delights my heart to watch the comments that come up as the day progresses. You know what I'm talking about, right? That game we usually play when someone manages to capture one of those life moments that you couldn't have staged if you tried.

Well, the title of this book is somewhat like that—*Worship Is...* and you fill in the blanks of what worship is to you. I have endeavoured to caption how my life has been shaped, impacted and given to what you and I call worship. For over twenty years, I have served in some capacity on worship teams and had the honour of pastoring many incredible worshipers and creative teams. I have had many 'caption this' moments along the way.

I've also endeavoured to caption the life of several heroes of our faith who model what a worshiping life is. My prayer is that my personal captions and experiences, and the stories that we find in the pages of the Bible, would help you to fill in your own blanks. Not just around what worship has been in the past, but what it could look like in your present, everyday life, and what it might look like in the future as you grow in your intimacy with Jesus.

So, before you read any further, take a few minutes now to 'caption this'. What is worship to you? Why don't you grab a journal or fill in the margin space right here and make some notes? You may find many adjectives or memories come flooding out of you. You may find it hard to describe, and feel stuck. That's okay. Give yourself the gift of time so that you can get the most out of the following pages. Invite the Holy Spirit to be present with you as you journal your very own caption of what worship is to you. Ready. Set. Go.

Start here—Worship is...

Okay... now that we've taken that step of self-reflection, let me share my dream for this book. My dream is that after you have read this book and reflected on its content, perhaps you might underline a few of the answers you just journaled, cross one or two out—or even add to the list. In other words, I want to challenge your perceptions of what worship really is, and in the process, perhaps we can grow together and learn from one another. I am confident that over the coming years, my own attempt to 'caption this' will grow, morph, develop and change. That's a good thing. Because in God, all healthy things grow with just a little bit of intention and a whole lot of grace!

I have attempted to write in a way where everyone—yes YOU—can feel like you've been invited over for coffee... and guess what? You don't have to audition!

You don't have to be part of a worship team. You don't have to be a 'good' worshiper. This is one size fits all. Come and get to know me. Just come as you are, sit on my couch, let's have a conversation and grow together in both our personal and corporate worship lives, which is the call of every single believer, whether you can belt out a tune or not.

Because I have such love and passion for building and imparting into worship teams, I have included a section just for you! If your main area of ministry or gifting is worship, you will find questions and a discussion guide in the back of this book for one-on-one discipleship, small groups, or worship and creative teams. The questions relate to common issues and growth points we face as worshipers and creatives. Together, you could caption some key learnings from each other's lives, perhaps from mine, and definitely from the Bible. (You can still do this even if you aren't involved in a worship team. The questions will help you to dive deeper and apply the content of this book.)

Now to take the pressure off the remaining chapters and set a good foundation, I have included some biblical definitions of worship right here in the introduction. After all, the only way to understand the practice of worship is to start with what God says worship is. Some of these definitions we will revisit in the following pages, others we will not. But to grow in our expressions of worship, we must grow in our biblical vocabulary of worship. So let's get to it!

WORSHIP IS
Biblical

Our English word 'worship' consists of two elements—'worth' and 'ship'. CS Lewis says that our natural response is to praise that which brings us delight.[1] This is what worship is—ascribing worth to God in response to a revelation of who He is and all He has done. It's delighting in Him with expressions of reverence and adoration. It is creation's response to the magnificence, power and goodness of God.[2]

Worship is not defined in one neat, simple story or a single Scripture or passage. In both the Old and the New Testament it is assumed that worship is the whole of our lives, which is why you can find worship woven through every book, every story and every life. It is the key biblical terms that are used for worship and their contexts, that therefore inform our concepts and understanding of all that worship encompasses—adoration, service and reverence.[3]

Throughout the Bible, worship involved listening to God's Word (for us today we have the privilege of reading it), prayer, song, work and sacrifice. Worship was offered in the home, at festivals, and in the temple involving both individual families and the whole nation of Israel.[4] Let's look at some of the key terms that help us understand what worship is. We'll start with the Old Testament.

Hawa: To bow down. This refers to bowing down in an act of worship, reverence or respect. It involves bowing down before someone who is superior, which was the custom in the ancient Near East as a sign of respect. This could involve bowing with the face to the ground or bending the knee. In worship, it was a sign of gratefulness and honour to a God who keeps His promises. An example of where this word occurs is in Exodus 33:10: 'when all the people saw the pillar of cloud standing at the entrance of the tent, all the people would rise up and worship, each at his tent door.' This describes a response to the manifestation of God's presence—to rise up, and then to bow down with their faces to the ground in worship.

Halal: To praise by listing out the positive attributes and actions of God. This form of praise often includes a shout or a song. We most often see this moment in our church worship services at the end of a song where we bring a 'shout of praise'. This isn't a mindless moment or just making noise. The power is in the intentionality of declaring *who* God is and *what* He has done. It is the natural response we feel rise within us whenever we see something great or awesome.

In Psalm 113:1–3, we see this word used five times: 'Praise the Lord. Praise the Lord, you his servants; praise the name of the Lord. Let the name of the Lord be praised, both now and forevermore. From the rising of the sun to the place where it sets, the name of the LORD is to be praised' (NIV). In a non-church context, you can see plenty of spontaneous *halal* at the football!

Tehila: This is a song of praise or adoration reserved for God alone. The lyrics of these songs, whether spontaneous or planned, describe the praise-worthy characteristics of God. These expressions of worship can also be shouted, but more often are sung in adoration to God. 'For as the earth brings forth its sprouts, and as a garden causes what is sown in it to sprout up, so the Lord GOD will cause righteousness and praise [tehila] to sprout up before all the nations' (Isaiah 61:11).

I love when I hear the church sing their *tehila*—spontaneous praise and thanksgiving to God in those free worship moments. These are the rare windows of time in our corporate services where we run out of someone else's lyrics, and we sing our own love song for all God has done for us in our personal lives—what a glimpse of Heaven! It's personal and it's intimate. This is a great expression of worship that can be best developed in the secret place.

Qarab: To draw near and approach God in worship. This indicates that we move in the direction of God. Often, this was the word used when someone brought an offering to God as an act of worship. It describes the sacrifices of the Levitical Priests on behalf of the people, which enabled the people to come close to God. This is one of those Old Testament worship terms that as a New Testament Christian, I can't help but read and just be filled with thanksgiving. Jesus, our

Great High Priest, has made a way for us to never have to go through the bloody and exhausting process of a priest sacrificing an animal so that we can draw near to God. Instead, Jesus is the once and for all sacrifice, and through His work on the cross, we become a royal priesthood. But hang on—I'm getting ahead of myself. That all comes later!

Rum: To lift up and to exalt God by declaring His accomplishments and attributes. This is a verb—a doing word that denotes moving things to a higher place. In worship, it is when we place significance on God for what He has done and therefore exalt Him. David sang this word in his song at the dedication of the temple: 'I will extol [rum] you, O LORD, for you have drawn me up and have not let my foes rejoice over me' (Psalm 30:1). Many of our praise songs do this and they are a wonderful foundation for God to move. As we exalt God, we dethrone anything that has taken His place in our lives and we put Him back on the throne of our hearts.

Zamar: To sing or play an instrument for worship. It is something that the Israelites often did in their worship of God, predominantly using stringed instruments designed for worship. It could also include the use of the voice as an instrument, making melody, *without* words, in reflection upon God's attributes and His salvation for Israel. Judges 5:3 says, 'Hear, O kings; give ear, O princes; to the LORD I will sing; I will make melody [zamar] to the LORD, the God of Israel.' I love this because often in worship, I hear the melodies of Heaven with no words. This doesn't make the melody any less powerful. In fact, sometimes pure melodic ministry is more inclusive, and therefore, more power-ful. Something shifts in the atmosphere when we echo Heaven's melody here on earth, whether it's through an instrument or a voice.

Abad: To work or to serve as an act of worship. It speaks of any regular task we do with an attitude of worship to God. This includes all secular work and our service to others. This word also described the work of the Levitical Priests in the tabernacle or the temple. Genesis 2:15 describes Adam's work in the garden as worship: 'The LORD God took the man and put him in the garden of Eden to work [abad] it and keep it.' It's worth noting that this is the first mention of worship in the Bible, and yet, often, our work is the last thing that we think of when we caption what our worship is. There's some food for thought.

As we move into the New Testament and examine the Greek words used for worship, we look at them in the context of Jesus having instituted a new way to worship. I could not possibly overstate how much this changed everything!

Proskuneo: To bow down and to worship as a sign of respect and 'to kiss towards'.[5] This is similar to the action described in the Old Testament word *hawa*. However, John 4:20–24 defines this type of worship as being given to God alone, whereas in the Old Testament, this bowing was the custom before any superior. Early Christians in the New Testament would often bow before God in prayer as an act of worship.

Paul also used this word when he wrote about what can happen when an unbeliever enters the corporate atmosphere of worship where the spiritual gifts are flowing: '...the secrets of his heart [the unsaved person] are disclosed, and so, falling on his face, he will worship God and declare that God is really among you' (1 Corinthians 14:25). What beautiful imagery these Scriptures depict as we bow our knee in prayer and worship and kiss towards the One our heart loves—whether it's an unbeliever's natural response to their sudden awareness of their need for God, or a seasoned Apostle such as Paul, bowed in prayer kissing towards his Saviour—it's stunning.

Eulogeo: To bless and to praise by showing gratitude to God. This is where we get our English word 'eulogy' from. In the New Testament, this is most often used to describe the worshipful act of magnifying God's mighty deeds. Jesus himself worshiped His Father this way: 'Then he ordered the crowds to sit down on the grass, and taking the five loaves and the two fish, he looked up to heaven and said a blessing [eulogeo]. Then he broke the loaves and gave them to the disciples, and the disciples gave them to the crowds' (Matthew 14:19). Eulogeo is irresistible to God. Notice that the miracle of provision in this passage came *after* eulogeo.

Sebo: To worship through acts of devotion to God. This was a word used in Greco Roman culture to talk about devotion to any god where the focus was on external performance to gain favour. However, in New Testament worship of the one true God, it is used to describe the 'awestruck' and devout Gentile converts throughout the book of Acts[6] where we read that '...many Jews and devout [sebo] converts to Judaism followed Paul and

Barnabas...' (Acts 13:43). Jesus warned against a focus on external performance when it comes to our worship, which we will look at in more detail in Chapter 8. This was a significant issue for this culture, and I believe it can be in our modern churches today too.

Threskeia: Ritual acts of devotion to a divine being. Paul warned the church in Colossae against threskia of angels.[7] In regards to worshiping God, it results in a change in the way we live life, shown in concern for others, that reflects God's character. James explained, 'Religion that is pure and undefiled before God the Father is this: to visit orphans and widows in their affliction and to keep oneself unstained from the world' (James 1:27). The service and concern for orphans and widows is an act of worship. Did you caption this one? We don't often think of loving orphans and widows as an act of worship. We more consider it an act of charity.

Kampto: Bowing as a sign of religious devotion in humility. Paul described himself this way in his letter to the Ephesians when describing his posture in prayer: 'For this reason I bow my knees before the Father...' (3:14). Here, Paul was literally bending his knee in prayerful worship. This is another example, similar to *proskuneo*, of an internal attitude that affects our external posture.

Doxazo: To praise and glorify God. In worship, this involves glorifying God in word or deed. In particular, when we model our lives upon the life of Jesus, we glorify and worship God: '...for you were bought with a price. So glorify God in your body' (1 Corinthians 6:20). We can worship God by offering our lives to Him as living sacrifices[8] and this brings Him glory.

We also bring Him glory when we reflect His character to others like mirrors: 'In the same way, let your light shine before others, so that they may see your good works and give glory to your Father who is in heaven' (Matthew 5:16). We also worship when we come together as a corporate body and worship Him shoulder to shoulder: 'When they heard these things they fell silent. And they *glorified* God, saying, "Then to the Gentiles also God has granted repentance that leads to life"' (Acts 11:18, emphasis added).

You can see from these biblical definitions of the attitudes and actions used to describe worship,[9] that worship is many different things. It is bowing and it is shouting, it is praying and it is playing instruments and singing. It is serving, working and taking care of widows. It's all of these things and more. The Bible captions worship in many different ways just through the various words it uses, let alone the stories it includes. With all of that in mind, come on the journey with me as I caption what worship is to me and as you continue to reflect on what worship is to you.

–1–

WORSHIP IS
Medicine

Music is the medicine of the mind.

JOHN A. LOGAN[1]

For as long as I can remember, music has been the calming influence in my life. As a child, I would lay down beside my dad's record player for hours and allow myself to be transported to another world by the melody, rhythm and artistry. I vividly recall, as a four-year-old, laying on my stomach beside those classic velvety, seventies record speakers for hours on end with my little ear pressed up tightly against the foam cover and weeping at the beauty of a Chess track called 'I Know Him So Well'.[2] The soaring melody. The tragedy in their voices. The bass line. The musicianship. I loved it all and I was hooked.

It's not like I could relate to the message of that particular song. At that young age, I didn't yet have a 'man to lose', nor did I look back and wish I'd played my love life differently. I was perfectly happy with my little life. I had no love life to angst over, and I could in no way relate to the message of the song in the natural.

But the melody—oh that melody! My parents would find me lying on the glorious shagpile carpet with tears streaming down my face, so moved by the beauty. And so my love affair with music began.

From then on and well into my teen years, I would spend hours listening to my older sisters' classical records, from Mozart to Beethoven and even Tchaikovsky. 'Moonlight Sonata' still makes me weep every single time. I would hide behind the couch as my mother taught piano and slide under the church pews as she taught the kids' choir their alto and soprano parts. I absorbed as much music as I could because it made me feel things that nothing else could. Music took me to other worlds and realms and caused emotions to rise in me that my little heart didn't even have the vocabulary to express. Music does that. In fact, most deeply spiritual things tend to. They bypass our intellect, our conscious, analytical and skeptical thought processes and journey straight to our hearts and spirits, evoking unrestrained responses of joy, sadness, longing and memory. It is God who created both us and music this way.

The Korahites were one of the principal families involved in leadership in the Jerusalem temple. They led the people in praise and worship and were temple singers from the tribe of Levi.[3] The Sons of Korah wrote many of the Psalms that we love to worship to today. In Psalm 42:7 they wrote, 'Deep calls to deep at the roar of your waterfalls; all your breakers and your waves have gone over me.' In my limited little heart and mind at the mere age of four, music was reaching to depths that I could not possibly know existed, causing the spring of tears to flow as deep called to deep and the breakers of His waves washed over me. And all of this to a Chess song!

I believe this happens because every human on the planet is made in the image of a creative and creating God, including Chess.

We are *all* His children, therefore whenever we create music and melody, whether we are in relationship with Him or not, we create because He made us to do so. We are like Him when we create. We reflect Him. We bear His image. So many artists strongly reflect the creative nature of God, but don't even acknowledge Him as their Lord. However, living separated from God does not alter the fact that they still create, because God gave them that ability. Their creativity is simply misdirected and less fulfilling—more about self and less about service. While the heart of the artist that composes the lyrics, crafts the chords, and pens the melody may not be directing their heart to God, it all still originates in Him because all melody and all artistry is a reflection of Him as the creator. Sure, the brokenness of the artist can often be heard in what they create, but that doesn't mean the person who created it is no longer His child. They just need Jesus!

Now when we find a surrendered life that loves God with all their heart, soul and mind that *creates*—there we find the most powerful and transcendent form of music and artistry there is—worship.

Just after I turned five, my mum and dad packed up all of their belongings (including the record player) along with their four children to embark on the adventure of a lifetime. We moved from a tiny country town in Victoria to a city that was humid, friendly, warm and yet scarily unfamiliar to me. We arrived just in time for my first year of primary school. To give you some context, the entire region and town I was born in was smaller than the suburb of Brisbane we moved to. This little farming community was only just larger than the school I was now going to attend. To say that it was overwhelming would be a great understatement.

Throughout that year, I suffered so badly with separation anxiety that I would literally kick and punch my teacher as hard as I could, as she peeled me—limb by limb—off my father. I was a tiny, weeny little thing, but my anxiety and fear were so great that my strength grew beyond myself to fight for the comfort and safety of my daddy's arms. I *hated* it. Every morning I would feel knots in my stomach and the dread of what was coming. I stopped sleeping well because I knew I had to go back there the next day. I would scream and cry as I watched my dad walk away with my little sister in the pram. This is where my journey with anxiety began.

Almost ready to give up after several weeks of warfare, my poor teacher came to a new school week with a last-ditch strategy to manage *my* growing distress and *her* fresh bruises. She soon discovered that placing me in a quiet corner, made comfortable with plump cushions and my own set of noise-cancelling headphones where I would listen to music, could calm me enough to join the class. Some days this took five minutes. On other days it took several hours. Eventually, the music would slowly unfreeze my timid and scared heart, calm my breathing, soothe my raging emotions, and give me courage and boldness to enter this scary new world that was before me.

Later in my schooling years, another teacher organised a music scholarship so that I could attend a performing arts school that our family could never have afforded any other way. I got to sing, dance and act for three hours every Saturday morning—it was bliss. I'm forever grateful to those teachers who persisted in discovering what worked for this little girl, amid the trauma that change and transition produced in me. These two women discovered, long before I had any self-awareness, that music could move me, bring me joy, comfort, peace, courage and even connect me to other places and times.

You can probably relate to this on some level. Have you ever heard a song on the radio or had one randomly pop up on your Spotify playlist, and you find yourself immediately transported back to a place and time long ago in your personal history—complete with all the emotions? From the song that played as you stole your first kiss or the dance track at your first blue light disco (totally showing my age here)—music and melody are powerful. Just ask my kids. As soon as the song 'Africa' by Toto (arguably one of the greatest drum and vocal tracks of all time) comes on, I am an instant dance party complete with air drums and embarrassing 'mum moves'. I can't control it. Whether I am in a shopping centre aisle or the local cafe, the music takes over as soon as that opening drum solo begins.

Songs can make us laugh or cry. They can convey someone's story with an emotional depth that words alone cannot. They can even have us attempting to dance—even if we really shouldn't! But in its most pure and sacred form, music is an art form given to us so that we can connect with our Creator, expressing in melody the truth of who we believe our God to be and what He means to us. Often, words are not even necessary, as melodies soar on vocal wings and communicate 'deep to deep'. In fact, the Israelites used melody, without words, to worship God on both stringed instruments and with their voices. It was called *zamar*. (You can read more about this in the introduction.)

When it comes to the science of music, a growing number of medical professionals consider music to be an effective inclusion in therapy as medicine. Several evidence-based studies support my own life experiences that there are numerous benefits for our well-being, health, the healing process and even our brain function simply by listening to music. These proven benefits include reduced anxiety symptoms, acceleration and improvement in the body's healing processes, improvements in the management of Parkinson's and Alzheimer's, improvement in depression symptoms and reduced disorientating symptoms of schizophrenia and other mental health disorders. Music therapy has been used to treat stroke victims, pre-term babies and in some hospital emergency departments, calming music is made available on Bluetooth speakers and headphones to help calm those who wait and to stimulate healing.[4]

In a nutshell, there is a change in our brains when we listen to music. Neuroscientists have documented that the band of nerve fibers that connect the left and right hemispheres of our brain (the corpus callosum) is thickened as a result of a healthy dose of musical medicine. This is the connective area of the brain that allows the two sides or hemispheres to communicate effectively. This connection results in almost every part of our brain being stimulated and activated in response to musical exposure. As far as these medical researchers can tell, there is no other human activity that engages as many parts of the brain as music! Music has the ability to wake our brains up, even after they have been suppressed or damaged during trauma, such as a stroke.[5]

Can we just take a moment and do a happy dance right now? Read those last couple of paragraphs again if you need to. Our creative God has provided us with the beautiful and powerful art form of music and melody and He has crafted it in such a way that it can heal us and redeem us from the fallenness, brokenness, sickness and disease of this world, from the inside out. It follows that when this art form is understood, redeemed, sanctified, anointed and directed to our Creator, its power becomes even more potent both for us as individuals and for those around us.

There is no other genre of music that has impacted my life as much as worship. I don't mean to restrict worship to just songs. Instead, I want to make it crystal clear that the songs we sing have a holistic affect on us. When we direct our hearts to God, rather than focusing on ourselves when we sing, it can bring us perspective and keep our minds and hearts focused on what truly matters and who we really are. When we worship, we are healed—body, mind and spirit! Don't ever let anyone tell you that worship is the warm-up in your church gatherings or that it doesn't matter in your personal life. Worship heals you. Worship frees you. Worship changes you physiologically, biologically and spiritually. Worship is medicine.

There was a man in the Bible known for his heart and skill in worship, who understood worship is medicine for ourselves and others. His name was King David. While he was still a boy, before he became the King of Israel, God made a way for him to use his skillful musicianship. It was perfected through hours of personal worship in the seemingly hidden places as a shepherd, and eventually led him to administer musical medicine to another famous but somewhat less noble king, Saul. Let's take a look at this profound biblical example of worship as medicine.

Saul was Israel's first king, appointed after the Israelites rejected God as their leader and asked the prophet, Samuel, to appoint a king to rule over them 'like all the nations' (1 Samuel 8:5). Even though this displeased the prophet, the Lord directed Samuel to give the people what they wanted—to anoint Saul as their inaugural king. King Saul had reigned for only two years over Israel before committing his first act of disobedience that, in God's eyes, disqualified him for kingship. Saul took the timing of God's will into his own hands and willfully disobeyed Him. This greatly displeased God, who sent a prophetic message through Samuel:

> 'But now your kingdom shall not continue. The LORD has sought out a man after his own heart, and the LORD has commanded him to be prince over his people, because you have not kept what the LORD commanded you.' (1 Samuel 13:14)

Even though God had already decided that Saul's kingdom was to end, He gave him another task, which was to take down one of Israel's long-time enemies, Amalek. There was one catch—he was given one very specific instruction. He must 'devote to destruction all that they have' (1 Samuel 15:3). He was to keep nothing alive. No animal, no man, no woman, no child—nothing! You would think that Saul would have learned to follow God's commandments exactly after his brush with impatience and disobedience. But no!

Saul gathered his army, set out against the Amalekites and defeated them. However, he did not completely destroy all that they had. Instead, he kept some of the choice animals and the best of their spoils for himself. Sigh. He also spared their king, Agag. Double sigh. The Lord spoke to the prophet Samuel again and said, 'I regret that I have made Saul king, for he has turned back from following me and has not performed my commandments' (1 Samuel 15:11). Seriously, Saul—you had one job! Saul had disqualified himself again through partial obedience, which exposed a divided heart. God sought a man who would serve Him wholeheartedly and He sent the prophet Samuel to find him.

Samuel was sent on a mission to the house of Jesse the Bethlehemite, where God told him he would find the new king. There was one major twist in the plot— Samuel had to act like 'Old Testament 007' because Saul was still reigning and he had some pretty epic anger issues. After seven of Jesse's sons pass before him, David, his youngest son, enters the scene. He was such an unlikely candidate that his own father didn't even ask him to come to the ceremony for presentation! He clearly didn't see kingship on his life. Thanks Dad! Instead, after first meeting all of his older, more qualified brothers, they called David in from minding the sheep in a field so that Samuel could see him. David was brought before him, and immediately the Lord spoke:

'Arise, anoint him, for this is he.' Then Samuel took the horn of oil and anointed him in the midst of his brothers. And the Spirit of the Lord rushed upon David from that day forward.
(1 Samuel 16:12–13)

Remember, all of this happened without Saul's knowledge. He was busy in his palace going all 'angry Snickers man' on everyone. In the very next verse, we read that 'the Spirit of the Lord departed from Saul' (verse 14). I believe this is one of the saddest verses in the Old Testament. Saul was so tormented by the anointing leaving him that a harmful spirit began to plague him. What was his servant's solution? Let's get a musician! He needs some musical medicine, stat!

As all the servants rushed around trying to find a remedy to calm their raging leader, one of the servants remembered that he had once seen a young boy named… you guessed it—David! He had seen him play the lyre and it just so happened that he was really good at it. (God was really bringing His A-game this day, wasn't He?) In a stroke of absolute divine genius, David is brought into the palace of King Saul to administer what Saul now lacked and longed for—the anointing oil that destroys the yoke[6]—and as we know, David had just been drenched in it by Samuel in a hidden moment!

The Bible says of David that King Saul 'loved him greatly' (1 Samuel 16:21). I believe this was because David carried and hosted what Saul had lost and grieved for. He longed for what was once so close to him that it had literally dripped down his own head[7]— the anointing of the Holy Spirit. But it was David who now carried this anointing, and when he picked up his musical weapon, he was divinely empowered to administer musical medicine to this wounded and grieving king. We read that, 'Whenever the harmful spirit from God was upon Saul, David took the lyre and played it with his hand', and Saul was 'refreshed and was well' as a result of David's anointed musician-ship (1 Samuel 16:23).

David's worship was medicine and it healed Saul momentarily from his grief and torment. It soothed him. It took him back to when he carried this same anointing. That's what music will do. You see, when music is administered by an anointed vessel that is yielded to God like David was, it is no longer simply music—it becomes worship. Sure, music can evoke emotion, connection and even take us on a trip down memory lane, but it is worship that can heal us from the inside out because it's only the anointing that breaks the yokes—not gifting or talent. It is here that we can administer healing to ourselves and others. Worship is medicine!

One of the greatest privileges of my role in the local church is that I get to pray with and for people. At our church, in every single one of our multiple weekly services, we open our altars during the worship time for anyone who has prayer needs. Each week, without fail, we see God's children flood the altar. Some need someone to stand with them and pray for healing, wisdom, relational issues, work pressures, or sometimes people come forward simply because they want more of Jesus. These are holy and significant moments that we value greatly as a church. As the worship team co-labours with those administering prayer ministry, there is a spiritual unity and authority that is released into the atmosphere. (More on that later.)

There have been times when I've asked the Holy Spirit what He might like to say to this son or daughter whom He loves so much, and I've felt Him lead me to sing over them. I remember one particular young lady plagued with insecurity and doubt. I watched her shyly approach the altar for prayer. The way her shoulders stooped and her feet shuffled, it looked as though she didn't even consider herself a worthy recipient of prayer ministry. I introduced myself to her and she quietly told me her name. I asked her what she would like prayer for but she didn't have an answer. In fact, she admitted that she didn't even know why she had come forward.

As I gently laid my hand on her shoulder and asked the Holy Spirit what He would like to do and say, the worship team hit a quiet instrumental section of a well-known song about our identity in Christ. 'Sing over her', the Holy Spirit whispered to me. To be honest, at first, I hesitated, but as I began to declare her identity in Christ and sing the words of 'Who You Say I Am'[8] over her, things began to shift.

I sang until *my* conviction grew, and *her* openness to God expanded, with a flood of tears and the humble posture of kneeling in submission to Him. I continued to sing over her until her spirit calmed and revelation soaked her heart. I could see it on her face and I could feel it in the atmosphere. That girl walked away from the altar differently than the way she had come. She walked away with her shoulders back, her head held high and with a new light in her eyes. *That* is the power of musical medicine. It was nothing to do with me. It was everything to do with the power of this medicinal gift of worship that God has given us that can transform and heal us physiologically, spiritually and emotionally. Worship is medicine. Have you had your medicine today?

– 2 –

WORSHIP IS
A Weapon

Satan is limited in every way. God gave him his gifts and abilities at his own creation. There has never been a battle between God and Satan. The entire realm of darkness could be forever wiped out with a word. But God chose to defeat him through those made in His own likeness—those who would worship God by choice.

BILL JOHNSON[1]

In 2017, I had the privilege of taking my fourteen-year-old son and a team of creatives, including dancers, photographers, musicians, singers and film editors, on a two-week trip to India. The purpose of this trip was to lead worship in Delhi and then visit a children's home in the eastern parts of India to capture on film, the amazing things God was doing there. It was during the second part of this trip to Odisha that we spent a day in the back of a Land Cruiser (think Meryl Streep in *Out of Africa* but in India) travelling to local villages to see what the support of our church had helped to build.

After several hours of touring local water wells and assisting an incredible team of workers with medical checks for the villagers, we arrived at our final stop for the day. We were the guests of honour, opening a brand-new literacy centre, recently built by a team from our church. To give context, this was a small room with a concrete floor where a teacher would live and sleep in the most basic conditions to serve the village children, teaching them to read and write. Alongside this was another concrete floor with a tin roof amongst the trees, coffee plants and deep red dirt where the villagers and children would gather daily to learn. Side note—it was so ironic to me that I spent the week surrounded by coffee plantations but could not find a good coffee anywhere!

This particular village was home to approximately 50–60 people, from newborn babies to a toothless 90-year-old grandmother who had much to say about the shiny new literacy shelter. As the whole community gathered, the women and children sat on grass mats on one side of the shelter; the men sat on the other side. My son and I were seated on the grass mats of honour at the front of the shelter where everyone could see us. I sat beside the amazing Matriarch who pioneered this work after visiting India and falling in love with the people. She went from being a local bank branch manager in Melbourne, Australia, to pioneering a hugely successful and life-changing community where children are valued, fed, educated, loved and taught about Jesus.

As the crowd settled under the shelter, an unexpected noise emerged from the bush. An elderly man, dressed in nothing but a thin, white, cotton nappy, approached the shelter shouting words that I did not understand—I still believe this may have been a good thing. The looks of distress and the subsequent yelling match that broke out amongst those gathered under the shelter gave me some indication that he was not blessing them with this native tongue! It was at this point that the Matriarch leaned over and whispered in my ear that the last time they visited this village, they were chased out with guns—GTK people! (Good to know!) The man continued to rant and rave, and the women yelled across the shelter at the men, and the men yelled back. As I began to have visions of being on the news in Australia for being killed in a small village in India, once again, the Matriarch tapped me on the shoulder and said one word—'Sing!'

'Sorry…what?!' I shot back. 'Stand up and sing something', she said as though it was the most obvious and natural thing ever. I nervously stood to my feet on the grass mat and sang the first thing that came into my head:

> You were the Word at the beginning
> One with God the Lord Most High
> Your hidden glory in creation
> Now revealed in You our Christ
> What a beautiful Name it is
> What a beautiful Name it is
> The Name of Jesus Christ my King
> What a beautiful Name it is
> Nothing compares to this
> What a beautiful Name it is
> The Name of Jesus.[2]

I know what you're thinking. Could I be more Christian? Surely, I could have chosen 'Eye of the Tiger' or the Rocky theme song to suit the situation. But as I sang that song with growing conviction and no instruments to accompany me, something began to shift. The nappied man began to approach the shelter and stare at me. Soon his yelling ceased. As I rolled on into verse two, tears began to stream down his weathered cheeks.

When I realised what God was doing, tears flowed freely down my face as I sang. By the time I got to 'You have no rival. You have no equal. Now and forever, God You reign',[3] you could have heard a pin drop as this man fell to the ground in the middle of the shelter and quietly wept. He couldn't even understand one word I was saying. Let me tell you it wasn't a flawless performance either—my voice shook with fear and emotion. You see, he wasn't weeping because of the beauty of my voice. He was responding to the beauty of the presence and the power of the name of Jesus. The presence and anointing of the Prince of Peace invaded that man's life and that open space, overcoming cultural barriers and whatever was causing his internal conflict. I still don't know what that man was yelling about that day or what was dividing that little community. What I do know is that it was all brought to peace and calm under that name—Jesus! Lucky I didn't sing 'Eye of the Tiger' after all!

I love how Dr Brian Simmons paraphrased the Apostle Paul's words to the church in Philippi about Jesus' name:

Because of that obedience, God exalted him and multiplied his greatness! He has now been given the greatest of all names! The authority of the name of Jesus causes every knee to bow in reverence! Everything and everyone will one day submit to this name—in the heavenly realm, in the earthly realm, and in the demonic realm. And every tongue will proclaim in every language: 'Jesus Christ is Lord Yahweh,' bringing glory and honor to God, his Father! (Philippians 2:9–11 TPT)

As I sat down, not quite comprehending what had just happened, the Matriarch leaned over with more good news—'You know you're not allowed to say the name of Jesus here, right? It's illegal. You can go to prison.' *Um. No. Are you allowed to sing it?*

I was humbled and so in awe of what had just happened. The angst and turmoil that man displayed in the coffee plantation was so unsettling for everyone surrounding him. It was undoubtedly a moment pregnant with spiritual unrest, and there was a war being waged for what we carried on our lives in the unseen realm. The spiritual climate and the powers and principalities that so visibly and tangibly reigned in that village and nation were getting nervous!

Just a few weeks earlier, a poverty-fighting organisation got evicted from that village and other villages all across that region of India. The spiritual warfare in this season and over this nation was and continues to be so real. And so this little western lady sang about the beauty, the wonder and the power of the name of Jesus, and every power and principality came into submission, and it didn't even matter that they had no idea what I was saying. Who knows, maybe it was the very first time they'd heard the beautiful, wonderful and powerful name of Jesus? Here's what I do know for sure: the name of Jesus caused every knee to bow, as this one life declared with all her strength, the authority and power in that name.

When we choose to worship (or when the Matriarch makes you) in situations that we don't understand or when we feel fearful, we engage with one of the most powerful and effective spiritual weapons of warfare that have been made available to us as believers. We know that 'we do not wrestle against flesh and blood, but against the rulers, against the authorities, against the cosmic powers over this present darkness, against the spiritual forces of evil in the heavenly places' (Ephesians 6:12). Satan is presented in Scripture as the ruler of the fallen angels or demons and this realm of evil.[4] He is called the 'god of this world' who has 'blinded the minds of the unbelievers' (2 Corinthians 4:4). He actually holds no authority over us as Christians or children of God other than that which we give him by agreeing with his accusations and lies.

When we allow him to steal our worship by even contemplating his lies such as God is not for us, God will not come through for us, or that we have reason to fear, we have admitted defeat. But, a confession of praise and worship confuses our enemy! He cannot understand a sacrifice of praise. In fact, he cannot stand it when we adore God and when we make much of who God is in our lives. Satan is an egotistical kleptomaniac who wants all our worship and who made a choice not to give his worship to God. He still desperately wants to be the object of your worship today and he is doing everything he possibly can to stop you from worshiping God because that would bring you down to his level and make you easier to defeat. But you are designed to be 'the head and not the tail' (Deuteronomy 28:13). Worshipping in the battle ensures you retain your spiritual position of authority and that Satan remains in his—under your feet with huge shoeprints on his head.

Satan was known as Lucifer in the Old Testament. Lucifer means 'light bearer'.[5] The story of Lucifer's fall was commonly known amongst the Canaanites and recorded in many historical and cultural documents of the day. His story is also broadly understood to be recorded in Isaiah 14:12. Lucifer was the morning star that attempted to rise high above the clouds and establish himself on the mountain where the gods assembled. His dream was to take the place of the highest god, becoming the ruler of the world. But because God is the only one worthy of praise and honour, He had to deal with Lucifer by casting him out of Heaven.[6] Jesus himself testified of this in Luke 10:18 when He said, 'I saw Satan fall like lightning from heaven.' Likewise, this was revealed to John on the Island of Patmos in Revelation 12:9: 'And the great dragon was thrown down, that ancient serpent, who is called the devil and Satan, the deceiver of the whole world—he was thrown down to earth, and his angels were thrown down with him.'

Satan wanted for himself that which belongs to God alone—our worship. And so, the war for our worship was birthed and continues today. Satan's entire role description is to steal, kill and destroy and to deceive us into believing that the weapons that God has provided for us to engage successfully and victoriously in this battle are not important.

I hear all the time that people can't wait for the praise and worship to be over so they can get to the real stuff like the preaching of the Word. When we believe these subtle lies, usually accepted because we feel like we're not particularly gifted at worship or because we don't personally like the stylistic choices of our corporate worship experiences, we lay down one of the most powerful weapons available to us that can bring the supernatural power and victory of God into our lives.

You may be facing a wall or a war in your life right now that can only be won through worship. The great thing is, the effectiveness of this weapon is not dependent on how well you sing or play an instrument (although if you're going to serve and lead the Body of Christ in this area, please love excellence), but it is contingent on the fact that you do respond in faith to the war that you are in, by declaring the goodness of God and His faithfulness, despite what your eyes may see in the natural. God can't help but respond to that kind of faith!

Jehoshaphat was thirty-five years old when he became king, reigning over Judah. He was a righteous king who walked in the earlier ways of his father David.[7] While David wasn't his biological father—Asa was—this was a reference to the fact that he sought God and walked in his commandments as King David did. This was a rarity during the days where kings reigned over the Israelites.

In 2 Chronicles 20:3–4, we get a glimpse into the character of this great king, when faced with a war against several invading nations. As the men approached Jehoshaphat to tell him of the incoming invasion, we read, 'Jehoshaphat was afraid and set his face to seek the LORD, and proclaimed a fast throughout all Judah. And Judah assembled to seek help from the LORD; from all the cities of Judah they came to seek the LORD.' Here we find a man—a king—with huge responsibilities and facing one of the biggest challenges of his reign, and his response to the fear he felt was to seek the face of the Lord, not to hang his head and agree with accusation, fear or doubt.

As Judah gathered together at Solomon's temple and entered a corporate fast, Jehoshaphat didn't begin by declaring or confessing the magnitude of his problem or what he needed from God—instead, he began with worship. He understood that once he got himself in the atmosphere of worship—which reminds us of our headship—his fears didn't stand a chance. His prayer begins by remembering God's faithfulness and exalting who He is over the reality in front of him. One of the words used for worship in the Old Testament is the word *halal*, which means to praise.[8] It's the act of listing and celebrating the positives attributes or actions of God. That is what Jehoshaphat did. He built his faith for the future based on what God did in the past.

Only after building this atmosphere of faith did he begin to pour out his petition before God, concluding his prayer with this statement: 'We do not know what to do, but our eyes are on you' (2 Chronicles 20:12). This little statement set Jehoshaphat up for the miracle that God was about to perform on his behalf. In the same way, when our situation is screaming at us to fix our eyes on what is happening in the natural, the breakthrough is set in motion when we fix our eyes on Jesus—the author and perfecter of our faith[9]—using the weapon of praise! In an atmosphere pregnant with possibility and charged with faith, the prophetic guidance that Jehoshaphat sought was revealed:

'Listen, all Judah and inhabitants of Jerusalem and King Jehoshaphat: Thus says the LORD to you, "Do not be afraid and do not be dismayed at this great horde, for the battle is not yours but God's. Tomorrow go down against them. Behold, they will come up by the ascent of Ziz. You will find them at the end of the valley, east of the wilderness of Jeruel. You will not need to fight in this battle. Stand firm, hold your position, and see the salvation of the LORD on your behalf, O Judah and Jerusalem." Do not be afraid and do not be dismayed. Tomorrow go out against them, and the LORD will be with you.'

Then Jehoshaphat bowed his head with his face to the ground, and all Judah and the inhabitants of Jerusalem fell down before the LORD, worshiping the LORD. And the Levites, of the Kohathites and the Korahites, stood up to praise the LORD, the God of Israel, with a very loud voice. (2 Chronicles 20:15–19)

As they bowed their heads with their faces to the ground, they have again assumed the posture of worship. To *hawa* was to bow down in worship, reverence and respect.[10] It was a symbol of submission, an act of worship and a physical sign of honour. Jehoshaphat postured his body in such a way that his mind, logic and what his eyes could see, were positioned lower to the ground than his heart, which he offered to God in worship. That is how we can wage war! We have to stop overthinking things and relying on our own resources and strength, and simply bow in submission and worship to God, allowing our hearts to connect with Him in simple trust.

But the praise party didn't stop there. The atmosphere went from glory to glory as the most skilled, excellent worship band of the day got up (the Levites were set apart for their musical ministry and commitment to excellence by King David) and began to lead the congregation in riotous praise! It made no logical sense to do this when facing the biggest battle of their lives. They should have been gathering weapons and strategising about ranks and supplies. But instead, they chose to love God and connect their hearts with Him over logic and what made sense at that moment, and don't we all know—God cannot resist that kind of worship!

It was common during times of war for armies to send spies into the lands they were planning to invade. While there is no written biblical evidence of this happening in this scenario, it is not unlikely given what we read of other battles throughout the Old Testament. I like to imagine that spies were sent in from the Moabites, the Ammonites, or the Meunites to spy, and that they stumbled across one heck of a noisy praise party! I'm sure that's not what they were expecting. I wonder if they left thinking—*Well this is going to be easy!* More likely, they left wondering where they could find that kind of peace, joy and faith in the midst of such adversity.

As I become somewhat of a spy as I read this passage about my patriarchs, I ask those questions. How did they manage this kind of outrageous faith in the midst of the largest battle they had ever faced? I suspect, just like you and I, they did it scared at first, and then as they stepped out, God grew their mustard seed of faith[11] into something that looked more like a praise party where everyone danced on the devil's head!

But just wait…it keeps getting better. This story just won't quit! They head out into battle early the next morning with their instructions received through the prophet, and there in the wilderness of Tekoa, Jehoshaphat gives them the heavenly and illogical strategy:

…And when they went out, Jehoshaphat stood and said, 'Hear me, Judah and inhabitants of Jerusalem! Believe in the LORD your God, and you will be established; believe his prophets, and you will succeed.' And when he had taken counsel with the people, he appointed those who were to sing to the LORD and praise him in holy attire, as they went before the army, and say, 'Give thanks to the LORD, for his steadfast love endures forever.'

And when they began to sing and praise, the LORD set an ambush against the men of Ammon, Moab, and Mount Seir, who had come against Judah, so that they were routed. For the men of Ammon and Moab rose against the inhabitants of Mount Seir, devoting them to destruction, and when they had made an end of the inhabitants of Seir, they all helped to destroy one another. (2 Chronicles 20:20–23)

Jehoshaphat arms his people not with weapons of earthly warfare such as shields, swords or strategy, but instead, he arms with them a song. He sends the worship team out at the head of the army, in front of the most skilled soldiers and commanders. He sent the singers before the rest of the army! Let's just take a moment because this isn't normal, nor is it the best or most logical military strategy. I don't know about the musicians and singers you know, but I don't know many who learn the art of warfare as a side hobby. And yet in God's economy and in the realm of warfare where the prize is to be the object of worship, the most effective warrior and the most effective weaponry is a worshiper with a song on their lips. And as these warriors took up their position, lifting their song of thanksgiving and praise to God, His supernatural intervention was released.

Some theologians believe that the ambush that God set as the worshipers sang, were angels in human form whose sudden appearance caused panic and confusion. Others believe that amongst these multiple tribes and nations that were coming against the Lord's chosen people, jealousies and animosities sprung up, which led to them turning on one another and lying in wait to ambush their own allies.[12] Either way, confusion reigned. You see, whenever God's people choose to lift a song of praise amid fear and opposition, it confuses the enemy, whether that be Satan or whether that be a vast army. The confusion leads to defeat in the enemy's camp, whereas the worshiper's focus on the goodness of God brings victory.

In true Jehoshaphat style, he gets the musicians to crack out the harps, lyres and trumpets back in the temple to celebrate their victory. (This was after they finished collecting more spoil than they could carry.) This man could not help but worship. It was his lifestyle. It was the key to his breakthrough. It was his most effective weapon in times of warfare. I love how Theresa

Dedmon reframed 2 Corinthians 10:4: 'The weapons of our warfare are creative, but we must make the choice to activate these weapons.'[13] Don't let the enemy tell you that you can only win the battle if your song is perfectly in tune.

Psalm 98:4 says, 'Make a joyful noise to the LORD.' The word 'noise' here means a public noise that signals feelings. It could be a verbal shout of worship or a song. It just needs to be a joyful, faith-filled noise! Your noise, if directed to God, is worship, and it's powerful.[14] Yes— even if you're tone-deaf, this applies to you. Don't lay down your weapon!

In Acts 16, we see another powerful example of the supernatural power of worship. Here we find Paul and Silas confined in a maximum-security jail cell, bound in stocks and chained to the wall. Essentially, the act that so offended the Romans and ruling powers of the time was that they exorcised a spirit from a tormented slave girl. The problem was, the evil spirit helped her to be a very effective fortune-teller. Once they dealt with the spirit, she could no longer accurately predict the future and had effectively lost her ability to produce an income for her owners. So, they seized Paul and Silas and dragged them before the magistrate and had them beaten and thrown in prison for disturbing the city.[15] It is here, beaten and sore and restrained in prison that we find Paul and Silas praying and singing. Yep.

Midnight.
In jail.
In pain.

Sore.
Bruised.
Broken.
Unable to move due to the restraints.
Praying and singing hymns.

Defies logic, doesn't it? I can imagine that the other prisoners' groans and cries for freedom were silenced by the unexpected sound of worship echoing down the dark hallways. Perhaps they thought they were total lunatics—often our worship in the midst of warfare looks like lunacy to others. But as we've already discussed, God finds this kind of faith stance and confession irresistible.

> About midnight Paul and Silas were praying and singing hymns to God, and the prisoners were listening to them, and suddenly there was a great earthquake, so that the foundations of the prison were shaken. And immediately all the doors were opened, and everyone's bonds were unfastened. (Acts 16:25–26)

Totally normal, right? A sudden earthquake that shook the foundations of the prison so that the doors were opened and their restraints were smashed to smithereens and yet the roof didn't collapse. Sure guys. Totally natural—*not*! It's supernatural. It was God's supernatural response to them picking up the weapon of worship, putting their head below their heart and filling their mouths with faith-filled confessions about who God was to them. Did they do it expecting the earthquake? I don't think so. I think they just loved on the Lord with hearts of worship, and in the process, they experienced His presence and power right in the prison cell and secured their supernatural freedom. Not only did they free themselves, but the door of *every* single prisoner's cell was opened through their worship. That's how big our God is. That's how much He loves it when we pick up the weapon of worship just because we love Him.

There is another word used in the New Testament to describe our worship of God. The word *proskuneo* that we find in John 4 where Jesus describes the type of worship the Father seeks, and it means to kiss towards. It paints the picture of a dog licking his master's hand with affection. The noun, *proskunetes*, is an adoring worshiper.[16] As Paul and Silas decided to sing to God and worship Him—to kiss towards their God, to adore Him despite their physical situation—it was irresistibly endearing to the heart of God. Not only that, but it was repulsive to their enemy who had attempted to steal, kill and destroy what Jesus had commissioned and given them authority to do. Here, Satan had to witness them not blaming God, not questioning God, but lifting their faces to kiss towards their Saviour. I can imagine him stomping away in frustrated defeat, as once again, the weapon of worship rendered his plans null and void, and he was reminded that he was under their feet.

There is a reason that the barren woman, who was a metaphor for the desolate and uninhabited city of Zion,[17] was commanded to sing:

'Sing, O barren one, who did not bear; break forth into singing and cry aloud, you who have not been in labor! For the children of the desolate one will be more than the children of her who is married,' says the LORD. 'Enlarge the place of your tent, and let the curtains of your habitations be stretched out; do not hold back; lengthen your cords and strengthen your stakes.' (Isaiah 54:1–2)

Notice that in verse two, the barren woman is commanded metaphorically to add on more living space in a home that is achingly empty. God had promised His people that salvation and restoration would come to them. How did they *make room* for this victory in their lives and hearts? By singing. By worshiping.

When you lift up a song of worship despite what your eyes see, despite what the doctor's report says, despite what you find yourself imprisoned by, despite the army that comes against you, you make room in your life for the fulfilment of the promises God has made to you. You defeat the enemy of fear, doubt and disappointment when you lift up a song of faith and focus on who God is rather than the obstacles you face. The enemy is left confused, and God cannot help but invade your heart, life and situation with His manifest presence that always brings victory. Worship is a weapon.

My question for you today is, will you use it? Maybe your breakthrough is just waiting on the other side of a song lifted in faith to God. Maybe it's on the other side of putting your head below your heart and bowing in worship. Maybe it's on the other side of making a joyful noise of worship and thanks to Him. Maybe it's on the other side of an illogical praise party where you make much of Him and little of the mountain you face. Maybe it's on the other side of singing a hymn in the midnight hour. Maybe it's singing a song before you have anything or anyone to fill the rooms in your home.

Here's what I learned in India and what I see in my Bible: lifting up a song of worship when you don't know what else to do and even when you feel completely awkward, is an act of warfare that disarms, confuses and defeats the enemy. It also feels good to sock it to him hard by giving God the one thing the enemy really craves—our worship. And in Jesus, the victory is already won. Have you got a song?

WORSHIP IS
freedom

True and absolute freedom is only found in the presence of God.

A.W. TOZER[1]

When was the last time you felt truly free? Was it when you were on your last holiday, free from the structure and expectations of your everyday family and working life? Was it the last time you had no debt? Was it before you had kids (aka, BC)? Was it when you were a child? Was it when you were at university? Was it when you lived at home, and your parents took care of everything for you? (Ah, the good old days.) Perhaps it was yesterday, and you're just living like William Wallace every day—yay you! Well, I was asked this question in a book[2] I read several years ago, and to be honest, my answer scared me.

I grew up in church my whole life. I'm a pastor's kid who has gone into the family business and is now pastoring herself for goodness sake. And we all know pastors have it all together, don't we? I'm serving God and have been for twenty years now. Shouldn't I be the freest person going around? (You can laugh. It's fine. I am.) Well, here is what I've discovered on my journey: even those 'happy-clappy' Pentecostals who freely dance and shout and jump for Jesus (of which I'm proudly one—I've got the t-shirt and hat), can still be bound up on the inside and not living in the fullness of the freedom that Christ has purchased for them. It's more common than you think.

The odd paradox of asking myself this question was that my honest and authentic answer went something like this: 'Do you mean outside of worship? Because I always feel completely free in worship, just not in my ordinary, everyday life.' And right there, began the journey towards making sure my life became more congruent in the area of freedom.

By this, I mean, how do we get to the place where we are just as free outside of worship as we are while in it—I mean, isn't this the very purpose of worship? To be so transformed, freed and changed in His presence from the inside out that it changes how we live our ordinary, everyday lives? If not, I am forced to face another hard question—is our freedom in worship a performance or just us 'playing church' with all the right moves? Or could those moments in worship actually be us at our purest, truest, most authentic, free selves and maybe, just maybe, the more time we spend worshiping this way, the more the rest of our lives will begin to reflect this? Either way, our freedom and our worship are more connected than we may like to acknowledge.

I haven't always been this free in worship. So, if you're reading this and you feel more free in your 'normal' life than you do when you are worshiping God, that's cool too. Maybe you're thinking, *But my personality isn't extroverted or emotional. My freedom may look different than yours.* Agreed! The way we celebrate our freedom is affected by our personalities to some degree, but we can't afford to use our Enneagram numbers as an excuse to mask the fact that we're actually still bound and not free before God! As Christians, our worship of God is meant to be so central that it directs all of the other areas in our lives. Another way to say this is that all of our life should flow *from* our well of worship. Conversely, if our worship flows out of a worldly culture that tells us who we are or emphasizes what we do, how much we have, and what our job title is—we are approaching things the wrong way around.

Let's make this really simple. When we worship, we're not worshiping as the CEO of a large company or as a nurse, a graphic designer or a chef. I'm not worshipping as a mother of four kids or a wife. I'm not even worshiping as a pastor. Gasp. Yes, those things might be our roles and assignments in life, but we're to approach worship simply as God's child—a child who has been set free because Jesus has set us free. We're not worshipping *for* freedom. We're worshipping *from* freedom. It is only when we understand this revelation that the rest of our lives can begin to reflect the freedom we have been awakened to in our worship!

Paul talks about this kind of freedom in Galatians 5:1: 'For freedom Christ has set us free; stand firm therefore, and do not submit again to a yoke of slavery.' I love that Paul says we *have* been set free. Not we *will* be set free. We have been. Again, we face this paradox—

if this is the case, why aren't we living free in every area of our lives? Well, Paul gives us the answer: we are still submitting to yokes of slavery in our lives every single day. Our role, with the help of the Holy Spirit, is to walk in the fullness of our freedom in Christ by identifying yokes and breaking free from them.

The imagery Paul used when he talked about this 'yoke of slavery' was often used in Jewish and Hebrew tradition, and therefore, Christian literature because of its easy relatability. It was an easy metaphor for the people of the time. Not so much for us today, so let's take a moment on this concept.

The yoke was a tool used to bind and control animals or human prisoners together. Slaves were often bound together by a large wooden rod across their necks; the yoke, attached by leather straps to ploughs. Their arms were tied to the sides of the bar, as they were forced to carry large volumes of water, hung on the bar in buckets and other vessels. Cattle were bound for productivity in the same way. In each case, it's important to note that yokes were instruments of production and symbols of slavery and submission.[3] Isn't that interesting given most of the areas we struggle to be free in or continue to be yoked to, are often related to what we produce? We become enslaved by our misplaced identity as producers or products.

Dallas Willard explains this in a much more profound way when he says, 'The most important thing in your life is not what you do, it's who you become.'[4] Failing to understand this results in submission to a yoke of slavery. Living this way often means it becomes difficult for us to approach God's presence from the position of having already received our freedom. You see, we bring our yokes of slavery with us into God's presence. We bring our yokes of production, misplaced identity, fear, pride, anxiety, insecurity or consumerism. (I'm sure you could insert your own struggle in there. We all have them—my list could fill this book.)

In my early twenties, I had the privilege of leading worship at a leaders' meeting for the church I was planted in, and I was so excited about it. It was kind of a big deal in the culture and context to be entrusted with leading this meeting at my age and stage of life. I loved to lead worship, and I loved the team and large vibrant church I was a part of. I knew it was such an honour to be entrusted with leading this night, but if I'm honest, I'd grown quite proud in my heart about the honour that I was being gifted with—both from God and my leaders. I accepted the lie that I'd done something to earn it.

In hindsight, I can see that I was using my worship-leading role to try to work my way towards freedom from insecurity. That's okay, God is kind and He doesn't slap us or embarrass us to teach us. Time and again, I can testify that God's great kindness has led me to consistent repentance,[5] to awaken in me increasing levels of freedom, discovering that my identity and security are found in Him, not what I do.

So this particular night, I'm ignorant of the fact that I'm carrying hidden pride in my heart. But God wasn't. So right in the middle of the worship set, I hear the Holy Spirit whisper to me, 'Stacey, I want you to run around the room.' Now maybe you're more sanctified than me, but I rebuked that thought and just kept leading according to my own agenda of how this whole thing was meant to play out and make me look good. Until… He kept on saying it to me over and over again—'Stacey, I want you to run around the room.'

So I did what any good worship leader would do and led the congregation to a moment of lifting hands and eyes closed to minimise my audience before I took off down the stairs and did what I thought would be a quick lap of the auditorium. I'm not talking a small auditorium here either. I'm talking about an 1100-seater with a slight incline. This wasn't even an easy run physically, let alone for my pride and ego.

So as I near the stage after my lap thinking, *Phew, not too many people saw me*, the Holy Spirit says, 'Go again!' By this stage, I'm beginning to enjoy the run, so I just keep going. I noticed that one of my best friends had joined me, and we ran like crazy people, laughing together. It was the most freeing thing I had ever done! I'm sure some people thought I was weird. Others wanted in and joined the run! Most people will have forgotten it even happened, but I could never forget what happened on the inside of me. I awakened to the truth that in Christ, I was set free from caring what other people thought or even said. I was learning to literally run in my freedom. I didn't have to earn it with a perfect performance. I already had it. I just had to learn to run *with* it!

These are the moments of awakening to our freedom that are available to us when we worship God, and they change everything! It broke pride and the fear of man in every area of my life. That's not to say I haven't struggled with it again. I have. It's one of the biggest giants we face when we worship—whether we're leading worship, worshiping in the congregation or even when we worship in the secret place of private intimacy that nobody else sees. King David was a man who had a similar experience of awakening to his freedom in God's presence. It's one of my favourite stories in the Bible, and it's found in both 1 Chronicles and 2 Samuel. Let's give ourselves some context to work with.

David was a man chosen by God, who rose from humble circumstances to lead the nation of Israel. During his forty-year reign, David led the capture of Jerusalem, established it as the capital, and unified the nation to build an empire of influence never seen before that stretched from Mesopotamia to Egypt. He was a shepherd, a musician, a poet, a warrior, a politician, an administrator and the standard for kingship.[6] David seemed to have it all. He was that annoying person with athletic prowess, musical ability and leadership. But the most important mark of David's life and the one that qualified him in God's eyes for leadership was that he was a man after God's heart.[7] This role of kingship came with quite a set of expectations and pressures. This is what makes David's freedom in worship all the more remarkable.

Now, let's talk about the significance of the ark. The ark of the covenant was the most important piece of furniture and symbolism that was built for the wilderness tabernacle that God instructed Moses to build.

It was an oblong chest made of acacia wood that was overlaid with gold inside and out and fitted with two pairs of rings through which poles would slide to make it easily transportable. As the Israelites moved, so did the ark, carried by the Levitical Priests. Inside the ark were the two tablets of the law that God gave to Moses along with a pot of the manna that God supernaturally provided to the Israelites in the wilderness and Aaron's rod that had budded as a sign of God's authority upon Aaron.[8]

The Israelites believed that the ark of the covenant was a symbol of Yahweh's earthly throne, which represented His presence on earth. It was the central symbol of God's presence with the people of Israel and is woven centrally right throughout the story of our forefathers.[9] It was always intended that all of life would flow from the presence of God, and therefore even in the old covenant, the physical ark that represented this presence is central to the story of the Israelite people.

Now that our context is settled, let's look at 2 Samuel 6 where David finally brings the ark into the newly established Jerusalem. This was a big deal and sent a very strong message about what was going to mark David's reign and how he was going to lead Israel. So David gathered 30,000 of his men and headed off to collect the ark that had been at the house of Abinadab for twenty years following its return from the Philistines.[10]

In verse 5, we read that 'David and all the house of Israel were celebrating before the LORD, with songs and lyres and harps and tambourines and castanets and cymbals.' In other words—they were part of a travelling worship service. Can you imagine it? The sound of tens of thousands of voices singing and celebrating to the accompaniment of the instruments that David himself had created to express his worship to God.[11] The problem was, in his zeal, David failed to follow the instructions to only transport the ark using the rings and poles and instead put it on a cart pulled by oxen. Sounds like the quicker and more logical option, right? Yet it wasn't what God had clearly prescribed, and David knew it.

In verse 6, we read that one of the oxen stumbled, and Uzzah (one of Abinadabs's sons) reached out to steady the ark and took hold of it. Immediately, Uzzah was struck down and killed. The party and celebration were silenced because of a stumbling ox, an attempt to steady or control God's presence, and an overly zealous king. David first responded with anger and then he recoiled in fear and abandoned his plan to bring the ark to Jerusalem, leaving it at the house of Obed-edom for three months.

In verse 9, we read, 'And David was afraid of the Lord that day…' One commentator believes that this fear David experienced wasn't a healthy fear of God, but a 'guilt-induced fear' that caused him to withdraw from God's presence in shame and embarrassment.[12] In other words, David went from being abandoned, joyous and free in his worship—to being yoked with fear, guilt, shame, and held back in his worship towards God.

I find it interesting that when David gained the courage to try once again to bring the ark into the city of Jerusalem, the very thing he sacrificed as part of the procession and celebration was an ox. Don't miss the metaphor here. In other words, the thing that had caused him to stumble back into slavery to fear and shame became the very thing he sacrificed as an act of worship. How many times have you and I recoiled from God's presence because we have stumbled back into slavery from things Jesus has already set us free from—guilt, shame, condemnation or control?

What if instead of yoking ourselves to these things, we made them our humble sacrifice and offering in worship to God, just like David did? What if we allow them to become a doorway back into our freedom, rather than a shut door that the enemy wants to use to separate us from God? What if we used these things that try to enslave us from entering God's presence as a child of God, and in worship, confess, 'I bring my fear to you. I bring my shame to you as an offering. I make myself and my fears a living sacrifice in your presence.' And in doing so, we reclaim our freedom?

After making his offering, 'David danced before the LORD with all his might' (2 Samuel 6:14). He was no longer just celebrating with songs and instruments. Now he was dancing as well. David was enjoying even more freedom in God's presence than he had before. Why? How? David took the thing that could have kept him from closeness and freedom in God and brought it as a sacrifice before God because he realised—I'm not worshipping *for* freedom; I'm worshipping *from* freedom. He could do that because, under the old covenant, he had made a sacrifice of an ox that was pleasing and acceptable before God, fulfilling the requirements under the law that allowed him to come into God's presence and celebrate, dance and sing.

For us today, Jesus is the once and for all sacrifice that Hebrews 10:19–22 talks about:

> And now we are brothers and sisters in God's family because of the blood of Jesus, and he welcomes us to come right into the most holy sanctuary in the heavenly realm—boldly and with no hesitation. For he has dedicated a new, life-giving way for us to approach God. For just as the veil was torn in two, Jesus' body was torn open to give us free and fresh access to him!
>
> And since we now have a magnificent King-Priest to welcome us into God's house, we come closer to God and approach him with an open heart, fully convinced by faith that nothing will keep us at a distance from him. For our hearts have been sprinkled with blood to remove impurity and we have been freed from an accusing conscience and now we are clean, unstained, and presentable to God inside and out! (TPT)

Because of everything Jesus has done, we are freed from an accusing conscience that could keep us from worshiping from freedom and enslave us into worshiping for our freedom. That should make all of us want to dance just like David did—although perhaps keep your clothes on. Come on! You should need to take a little praise break right now! Do a lap of your room if you want. I won't judge.

Isn't it sad how Saul's daughter and David's first wife, Michal, responded to David's freedom in God's presence?

> 'How the king of Israel honored himself today, uncovering himself today before the eyes of his servants' female servants, as one of the vulgar fellows shamelessly uncovers himself!' And David said to Michal, 'It was before the LORD, who chose me above your father and above all his house, to appoint me as prince over Israel, the people of the LORD—and I will celebrate before the LORD. I will make myself yet more contemptible than this, and I will be abased in your eyes.' (2 Samuel 6:20–22)

Michal seemed to inherit her father's inability to humble himself in worship and submission. In her eyes, there was a set of expectations that went with being a dignified king, and dancing around half-naked wasn't one of them. Michal exposed her own struggle with freedom in her response. She was bound and yoked, restricted by misconceptions of what she thought things were supposed to look like and fear of what others might think about her. She was a queen by title, but a slave in her heart to fear and shame, and this slavery that God never intended her to live in resulted in an internal bitterness that never allowed her to produce natural fruit.[13]

Slavery always brings death. Freedom always brings life. Don't you just love David's response to her projection? Eugene Peterson paraphrases his response this way: 'Oh yes, I'll dance to God's glory—more recklessly even than this. And as far as I'm concerned… I'll gladly look like a fool' (2 Samuel 6:22 MSG). You see, a person awakened to their freedom doesn't really care what anyone else thinks! They only have eyes for the person who purchased their freedom. He becomes their audience of one.

And so we return to the question I opened with: when was the last time you truly felt free? Exhausted with the wrestle of seeking to find answers to this question myself, I fell onto my pillow late at night after two weeks of questioning, and I cried out to God and said, 'God, how can this be? Why can't I remember my last true expression of abandoned freedom outside of worship?'

Immediately, I was transported back in a vision to a time when I was just five years old—brand new at school in a new city where I knew no one, struggling with anxiety and fear—which we already discussed. Alone each lunch hour, I would skip around the beautiful Jacaranda tree and enter my own little world where it was just Jesus and me. I skipped and I skipped and I didn't care what anyone else thought. Now well into adulthood, I spent the next couple of years working through what it would look like to recapture that free little girl that didn't care what anyone else thought and could freely skip to her own beat and just enjoy Jesus.

The moment of awakening came as I led our church in worship at our annual conference. I had come through a very challenging season where I felt particularly restricted and boxed up in many areas of my personal world. It was frustrating, and I didn't know how to break out of the shadows I felt engulfed me. I felt unable to talk to anyone about it and alone in my inner turmoil and frustration. During this time, I believe God allowed this heightened sense of restriction to gently guide me to rediscover and reawaken to the freedom of the skipping girl I was born to be. It was a motivator of sorts.

It was at this conference, two years after being asked that freedom question, that our church was in a very sacred and holy moment of surrender and repentance. We had just sung the words of the Cody Carnes song, 'I'm sorry when I've come with my agenda. I'm sorry when I forgot that You're enough. Take me back to where we started. I open up my heart to You.'[14] And then we waited... on our knees in the quiet. We just waited. It was holy, and it was beautiful.

As I bowed on my knees on the platform in front of my church family, together in a sacred moment that would mark each of our lives, I heard that whisper once again that I had learned twenty years later to obey quickly rather than rebuke. I love how Dan McCollam puts our willingness, or lack thereof, to obey the voice of the Holy Spirit:

You are currently moving at the speed of your own obedience. How many times does it take you to hear from God before you respond? Does it take three impressions, two Scriptures, a prophecy and four confirmations? Then, that will be the speed of your growth.[15]

I want to obey the first whisper and I am getting better at this, so when I heard, 'Stacey, get up and skip before me', I did not hesitate.

During that holy, sacred moment, I awakened to the freedom that had always been mine but I'd neglected to walk in for more years than I care to confess. So I skipped. I skipped up and down that stage like my five-year-old self. I ran and I danced and I skipped. Tears streamed down my face as I awakened to my freedom and I let go of all the yokes that I had allowed to enslave me for way too long. Guess what broke out in that room? Freedom. The church spontaneously rose from their knees one by one and celebrated the freedom of their fresh forgiveness. I'll never forget it. In the same way that I believe King David's abandonment before God would have caused other people to think, *Well if the king can dance and sing, so can I,* the awakening of freedom in me gave permission to others. I want to spend my life living and leading that way.

The day after our conference, a very dear friend and fellow leader who I respect and love very much, Ps Raef, sent me this text message:

When I saw you run and dance on the platform, I felt God speak to me about you and the church. I saw the Spirit of God blow on you as you ran, and like a flower that was once bent down, you immediately blossomed and the colours in you were so diverse and radiant (really high definition) and the fragrance which came from the blossom literally made all who inhaled it come to the same life. And I heard God say that he was freeing the child Stacey and in her child state she would be used to free multitudes.

I weep all over again even as I put this testimony of my own reawakening to freedom on paper because I am so grateful to God for the reality of John 8:36 lived out in my life—'So if the Son sets you free, you will be free indeed.' He knows every detail of our lives and He knows how to weave it all together for His glory and for our good. At this moment, I was truly worshipping *from* my freedom and not trying to earn what was already mine.

Worship is freedom. It is not a pathway to gain freedom; it's an experience of connection with God where the heart is awakened, over and over again, to the freedom that is already ours. We are freed and released from the things we yoke ourselves to because, in His presence, we are awakened to the truth of what is going on in our hearts. And that recognition of the true state of our internal world won't crush us or lead us to wallow in condemnation. That's just not the way my Jesus works!

Jesus says, 'the truth will set you free' (John 8:32). The true state of our hearts and our constant struggle with slavery will awaken us to the freedom that is ours because of the price Jesus has already paid: 'The Lord is the Spirit, and where the Spirit of the Lord is, there is freedom' (2 Corinthians 3:17). This speaks of the presence of the Holy Spirit and how His presence awakens us to our freedom.

Psalm 100:2 encourages us to 'Come into his presence with singing!' In other words, when we worship, we can bring ourselves into His presence with a song. And here, in this place of surrender and connection with God, we are awakened to our freedom. Worship is freedom!

WORSHIP IS
Stillness

Be still, and know that I am God.

PSALM 46:10

There is a common misconception in our twenty-first-century consumerist culture that tells us that being still is to stagnate. Jesus teaches us in His Sermon on the Mount in Matthew 5 that although we may have 'heard it said' that something is true—by cultural leaders, commentators, or even the Church—the Kingdom of God often presents contrary truth. These Kingdom realities are invitations to live a better and more effective, fulfilled kind of life for God. The Bible is very clear that to be still is not to stagnate, but it is an essential component of our spiritual formation and growth. To stop and be still in God's presence and to worship Him by acknowledging that He is God and we are not, is super vulnerable, but vulnerability is necessary before God for true spiritual maturity to be present in our lives.

Mark Buchanan, in his book *The Rest of God*, says, 'Some knowing is never pursued, only received. And for that, you need to be still.'[1] James W. Goll says this of stillness, 'We cannot fully realise true intimacy with God until we learn how to come before Him in quietness of spirit, mind, and body. An atmosphere of stillness is absolutely essential for us if we wish to experience deep, loving communion with our Lord.'[2]

Psalm 46 is one of the collections of six 'Zion songs' that we find throughout the book of Psalms. They are hymns of praise focused on the location of Zion or Jerusalem, which became the capital of all Israelite life and worship under King David's reign. This was the location where Solomon, David's son, completed the building of the magnificent temple that housed God's presence and was known as a place of connection between God's heavenly and earthly realms.[3]

This particular Zion song was written by well-known songwriters of the day—the Sons of Korah, who we spoke about in Chapter 1. The notes in the title tell us that this little hymn was to be played 'according to Alamoth', which indicated that the song would be sung with the accompaniment of the harp.[4] I don't know if you've ever heard a harp live, but it is one of the most beautiful and restful sounds you will ever hear. It is the perfect backdrop for the focus and intent of this worship song that speaks of God as our place of refuge and our protector.

In this particular Psalm, the writer begins by declaring in song some of the things he knows to be true about God and then observes some of the natural catastrophes such as earthquakes, stormy waters and unstable mountains to highlight God's power and sovereignty over creation.[5] The intent of confessing these attributes of God in a worship song is that the worshiper is left filled with courage and faith in the face of adversity. How many times has this happened to you in worship? You go in feeling like your problems are overwhelmingly huge, but as you lay them aside, focus on Jesus and sing about His faithfulness and goodness, He gets larger, and the issues of our lives are given an accurate perspective. I like to say it this way: praising God will change your internal and spiritual position, and changing your internal and spiritual position will change your perspective. Praise. Position. Perspective.

As the song continues to contrast the raging of nations, the rise and fall of kingdoms, and God's supreme strength, power and sovereignty, it all comes to a climax in verse 10, where we are told to, 'Be still, and know that I am God.' The word 'still' in this passage is the Hebrew word meaning release or let go.[6] The word picture painted for us in the context of the whole song is that God has the power to command the nations and the forces of chaos to stop their raging and recognise Him as God.

The personal application for us is that we are to do the same—release and let go of our chaotic and manic schedules and lives, the inner raging and the external forces that are out of our control, and simply recognise that He is God and we are not. The inference in this Psalm is that if we don't stop and make ourselves still, we will fail to acknowledge all the ways that God is moving, ruling and reigning in our lives. Therefore, our worship lives are diminished. How? Let me explain.

There is a spiritual principle present right through-out the Scriptures that teach us that God is always the instigator, and we are the respondents. He sends Jesus to rescue us; we admit we're lost and need saving. He loves us; we love Him and others. He speaks; we follow. Now when it comes to worship, He reveals; we respond. Fresh revelation corresponds to fresh worship. One commentator defined worship this way: 'the interrelation between divine action and human response'.[7] Living our lives in response to God is worship. We have been wired and created to respond freely and with thanksgiving and appreciation when we see something we like or that impresses us. This particular spontaneous kind of response in worship is called *halal*, which we covered in our introduction. Let me tell you about a particular season in which *halal* prevails in my own family.

There is a momentous annual occurrence in my house known as March Madness. For those of you who don't know, March Madness is the annual National Collegiate Athletic Association (NCAA) basketball tournament where several rounds are played in the lead up to the 'big dance' where sixty-eight teams are reduced to two grand finalists. It is a time of great importance in our house for my husband and three teenage boys. It is also a time of great spontaneous response and adulation as the latest star recruit 'does his thing' (think Zion Williamson). I knew when that boy had the ball in his hands because all four men in my house were on their feet, clapping, yelling and hollering! This was their spontaneous response to Zion's apparent greatness (insert motherly eye roll). But this is a great example of how we are wired to respond to greatness. When we truly catch a glimpse of who God is, we will not be able to hold back our response unless we intentionally do so. The problem is, revelation is not often caught on the run. The deepest revelations of the presence and the greatness of God in our lives, come in the stillness. None of my family (except for my daughter Eden and I) walk past the TV while March Madness is on. Those men are parked in that TV room and they are not moving. This is what it takes to see greatness and then respond.

When it comes to true worship, it is all response—to the greatness, majesty, faithfulness, goodness, sacrifice and love of our Heavenly Father. Often we find responding to Him more vulnerable and challenging than we do to other things in life, but the spiritual principle remains. Worship in its purest state comes down to this: God reveals; we respond. If our worship is not a response, we fall into the trap of 'playing church' or a spirit of performance.

Let's jump back to our Psalm for a moment. Throughout the Psalms, you may have noticed a little italicised word to the right of the Scriptures—the word *selah*. It appears three times in Psalm 46. Throughout the 150 Psalms, it appears 71 times and three times in the prophecy of Habakkuk.

Selah is a musical term that means to pause in silence.[8] Some scholars believe that this was a time where the worshiper would fall prostrate on the ground[9] in response to God. The dictionary definition of stillness is the absence of movement or sound.[10] In other words—*selah*. What is important to note is that times of stillness and silence to reflect on God's character were an important and normal part of the Israelites worship life. In the same way, it should be a normal and important part of our worship lives today. How can we ever truly live in response to something if we don't pause, make our inner dialogue silent, and simply *selah* in His presence? Some of the most powerful moments of both corporate and personal worship that I have ever been part of have been the moments where I have simply paused in silence to receive revelation. And if it's genuine, it will always lead to a response of worship.

Psalm 37:7 calls us to 'Be still before the LORD and wait patiently for him.' The Hebrew word used here is the word *damam*, which means to 'stand still' and to 'keep quiet'.[11] Again, here we see this principle of stillness as a part of our worship lives.

I have to admit that being still is not my natural strength or wiring. I love to be moving and doing. So to incorporate stillness into my own worship life and in my worship leading has been a journey. To be honest with you, I have only really discovered the richness and fullness of this practice in recent years and it actually took near burnout—physically, spiritually and emotionally—for me to learn to be still.

Let's just say, I must be a slow learner because I had already experienced eighteen months of Chronic Fatigue Syndrome (CFS) in the first two years of my twenties. I'm not trying to diminish the physical things that were going on in my body during that season, but God was arresting my attention in a very powerful way by making me lie down and rest. It was during this season of CFS that God realigned my life to ministry and back into an intimate relationship with God rather than the career and lukewarm life I was actively pursuing.

I am almost embarrassed to say that as a fresh-faced twenty-year-old, I had to reach the point of not being able to move—a forced stillness of sorts—for me to hear God's voice. I lacked understanding of the truth in Wayne Muller's words: 'Rest is an essential enzyme of life, as necessary as air. Without rest, we cannot sustain the energy needed to have life. We refuse to rest at our peril—and yet in a world where overwork is seen as a professional virtue, many of us feel we can legitimately be stopped only by physical illness or collapse.'[12] Ouch! Does anyone else feel that with me?

I've tried to grow in this area of my personal life and my spirituality, but I haven't always found it easy. I'm learning that the most rewarding and valuable treasures in God are usually the hardest to discover because we have an enemy that doesn't want us to grow in spiritual stature and weight. This is the reason that four years ago when I began to feel that I was approaching another round of running around the same old mountain of physical and spiritual exhaustion, it was a huge wake-up call for me. What did the Holy Spirit say to me? Two little words: *Study Sabbath*. Ever since that point, a weekly, biblical Sabbath that incorporates stopping, resting, delighting and contemplating God has become my lifeline and my greatest joy. I'm still learning about it and continuing to grow in this spiritual practice, but stillness and silence are a huge part of this sacred sanctuary in space and time[13] that God calls Sabbath.

There are facets to the diamond-like nature of our triune God, particularly in the realm of the supernatural and prophetic experience that I could not have discovered any other way than by stopping to know that He is God and I am not. As a singer and musician, this next statement is a huge one for me—musicians, songwriters and singers, put your seatbelts on! I have experienced more of the depths of God and the heavenly realm, some things too intimate to speak of, in stillness and silence—greater treasures than I have ever discovered, amidst even the greatest worship song. There, I said it! It's a big call, I know, but sometimes the *selah* is greater than the noise.

There are two sisters in the Bible who represent the perfect imagery of this tension we sometimes wrestle with when it comes to stillness. In Luke 10:38–42, we are given a bird's-eye view into the sibling inner sanctum of Mary and Martha. To help us paint a good picture in our mind of what the sisters' tiff that Jesus ended up in the middle of looked like, here is Dr Brian Simmons account:

As Jesus and the disciples continued on their journey, they came to a village where a woman welcomed Jesus into her home. Her name was Martha and she had a sister named Mary. Mary sat down attentively before the Master, absorbing every revelation he shared. But Martha became exasperated by finishing the numerous household chores in preparation for her guests, so she interrupted Jesus and said, 'Lord, don't you think it's unfair that my sister left me to do all the work by myself? You should tell her to get up and help me.'

The Lord answered her, 'Martha, my beloved Martha. Why are you upset and troubled, pulled away by all these many distractions? Are they really that important? Mary has discovered the one thing most important by choosing to sit at my feet. She is undistracted, and I won't take this privilege from her.' (TPT)

Let's take a moment to look at the posture of Mary. Mary was found sitting at Jesus' feet. Now, this was significant because to sit at the feet of a Rabbi indicated that you were one of his students or disciples. Mary had assumed the posture of Jesus' disciple.[14] It was radical for a woman in her culture to do this (which makes me love Jesus even more), and we need to notice this because, as disciples of Jesus, we too must sit in stillness to learn and mature into the fullness of Christ. We can't fully mature on the run! Let me say that again—*We can't fully mature on the run!* Did you read that on the run?

Stop for a moment.

Make your body still and then maybe say this out loud—*I can't fully mature on the run!*

Let's now look at Martha and how she approached the presence of Jesus in her home. I don't want to throw shade at Martha. I've been Martha. I think we all have. We read that 'Martha was distracted with much serving' (Luke 10:40). This word 'serving' is the Greek word *diakonia*, which is a ministry role or position of service.[15]

I can't even tell you how many times I've been so busy doing things *for* Jesus that I missed the invitation to just be *with* Jesus. I can also recall several times when I've prayed prayers like, 'God, I'm just so busy doing what you've called me to do that I can't seem to find time to read the Bible or worship you.' I don't think I'm alone here, and neither was Martha.

It is good that we desire to serve and love the Lord. However, in a world and culture that teaches us our value comes *because* we produce, prioritising the unseen work of our inner world and sitting at Jesus' feet in stillness to absorb every revelation He shares becomes difficult. It's also the path of delayed gratification in a world of instant fixes. Jesus, in His kindness, responds to Martha with such love and speaks to the culture of distraction that existed for her, and certainly exists for us today.

Do you ever have trouble focusing in worship? Do you ever have trouble focusing when you pray? Do you ever find it difficult to be still like I do? These are things that we must practice so that we can mature in them. The more we make ourselves still, the easier it becomes. The more we pray with focus, the easier it becomes. Don't be discouraged if you find this difficult at first. Your personality may find it more difficult than others. Mine did! But I'm telling you, 'one thing is necessary'.[16]

'Mary has discovered the one thing most important by choosing to sit at my feet. She is undistracted, and I won't take this privilege from her' (Luke 10:42 TPT).

Do you, like Martha and like me, need to make a conscious decision to lay aside anxiety and distraction to be still, and take the posture of a disciple at Jesus' feet? Worship is stillness. It's an act of submission and recognition of God's sovereignty in our lives to cease all activity, to focus on God and to respond to the revelation we receive in His presence.

Dallas Willard made this observation about stillness and silence: 'but silence is frightening because it strips us as nothing else does, throwing us upon the stark realities of our life'.[17] I have noticed in my own life and my endeavours to grow in this area that if I can stay busy, I can avoid and drown out my fears around not being enough for everyone or in anything. But am I really living if I never face those fears? I have concluded that this would not be living an abundant life, and I have chosen in the last few years to do the hard work of facing these fears that I'm not enough for my kids, not enough for my husband, not enough for my team and not enough for God. Ironically, I have found in the stillness that I don't need to be enough because Jesus is *more* than enough for me and His strength is made perfect in my weakness.[18]

Here's the thing: staying busy to avoid facing all we mask our lives with and the 'never enough' thoughts that run rampant in our heads, will cap our growth in Christ. We can come into His presence and worship

Him with all of our doubts, fears and questions—and the beautiful thing is, He won't leave us there. There is safety and transformation in the stillness of God's presence. Proverbs 18:10 says, 'The character of God is a tower of strength, for the lovers of God delight to run into his heart and be exalted on high' (TPT).

In a society of workaholics where busyness is worth and the prize, we have hardwired our bodies to be averse to stillness. When we consistently overwork, we affect the neurochemistry of our brains that release hormones and chemicals to meet the daily challenges we face. We become accustomed to living with, and eventually, become dependent upon these chemical releases. At its worst, this can result in clinical adrenal addiction.[19]

I get so mad when I think about how much the enemy attempts to rip us off from the fullness of experiencing Christ in worship and how many of us fall for it without even realising. The great news is this: you can reverse engineer this wiring in your brain and soon come to love your times of stillness in worship. Guess how? Psalm 46:10—'Step out of the traffic! Take a long, loving look at me, your High God' (MSG), or more simply put, 'Be still, and know that I am God.'

In the same way that there are things we cannot receive as a revelation about God without learning to be still, there are responses in our worship we cannot offer or express to God while we stay on the move. In Ephesians 6, Paul teaches us how to arm ourselves for the spiritual war we face, and once we have taken up the whole armour of God, he tells us that we should 'stand firm' (verse 14). In other words, we are told to be still.

One particular scholar reflecting on Psalm 46:10 writes that to 'be still' means to 'desist from our war'.[20] It is a bold statement of faith and confidence in the protection and sovereignty of God to make ourselves still amid the war we face, to desist from war, and trust that He will be our justice and our defender. Let's never confuse stillness with being static, stuck or stagnate.

Stillness in a world that never ceases is faith. It is an act of worship. Do you believe that you can trust God with your life? One of the ways we respond to this conviction is by standing firm or being still in His presence. Worship is stillness.

WORSHIP IS
Pneuma

Religion can be the enemy of God. It's often what happens when God, like Elvis, has left the building. A list of instructions where there once was conviction; dogma where once people just did it; a congregation led by a man where once they were led by the Holy Spirit.

BONO[1]

Ever heard the term Baptecostal? It's a combination of two words that are rarely put together—Baptist and Pentecostal. Some people might say this is an oxymoron. Others might say these two words should never go together. Or perhaps, if you're like me, you would say this is a great description of your denominational background and experience.

In reflection, it is a more apt description of my home environment than it was of my childhood church experience. You could call my parents closet Baptecostals. It's not that they were hiding anything intentionally; there just weren't forums for expression in our church structures for it to ever be on full display. Perhaps they were more 'bathroom Pentecostals' than 'closet Pentecostals'. You know what I mean? No one wants to know what you're doing in the bathroom, and they certainly don't want to join you there, but they're fine if you go.

I saw my parents listen to the voice of the Holy Spirit and live and lead according to this every single day. They had vibrant, healthy prayer lives and would often bring encouraging words to people based on words of knowledge they had received. My dad faithfully preached what the Holy Spirit told him to preach in prayer, and I got a bird's-eye view of his faithful exegetical study and presentation of God's Word. My mother, who is a psychotherapist, often followed the promptings and loving disclosures from the Holy Spirit to help people find wholeness and restoration in their lives. They encouraged each of us, five children, to do the same thing and often asked us what we thought God was saying and doing. I just thought this was normal!

As a child, I didn't realise there was an in-congruency between how my family's faith was expressed and lived out in our home, and how others we did life with and loved within the church family felt about the Holy Spirit. And I found out the hard way—the crash-landing kind of way. Let me start from the beginning.

I was the kid who loved to get up early every Sunday morning and sit in the back of my dad's Suzuki Swift as he drove to church. I loved listening to him practice his sermon during the twenty-five-minute drive it took to get from home to our church building.

It was on one of these mornings that we drove past a just completed, contemporary, progressive, multistory building close to our church. This was during the late 80s when I was about ten years old and I had never seen a building like it. It was architecturally very interesting and built along the edge of an amazing green belt that ran right through several inner-city suburbs of Brisbane.

As we drove past the office building and underground carpark, which would house a new up and coming IT business, I just knew that building would one day be our church. In fact, I thanked God in my own childish words for the IT company that built the building just for us. How did I know to do this? I'm not sure. I had no idea what was going on spiritually at that moment—it just felt as natural as breathing to me.

I casually interrupted my dad from his sermon monologue and said something along the lines of, 'That building is going to be our church one day. Isn't it great they built it for us?' He was pretty engrossed in his sermon preparation and didn't pay much attention. But every week following that moment, for the next eight or nine years, as we drove past that building on our way to church (sometimes we drove past it six times per Sunday between the to and fro), I would gaze at it with excitement wondering when it would finally be ours.

Let's fast forward to my late teens. By this time, my mum and dad had moved from being the youth pastors to leading the church as senior pastors and by the grace of God, it was thriving and growing. We were seeing radical conversions, including people out of the church of Satan (that's a whole other book), and God was doing some very powerful things in and through

Mum and Dad's ministry. Their church was becoming a real home for many young families and God was reviving people's hearts in powerful ways. But isn't it true that growth often brings with it the pain of necessary change, and people process this very differently?

Our church building was a well-known heritage-listed building, complete with a stunning pipe organ. The problem was, we were outgrowing it because of what God was doing. So the church leadership began to pray about what we would do.

It was during this season of prayer and seeking direction that one of the elders (who alongside his wife also happened to be my parents' closest friends and a big part of our family) received a prophetic message from God about what we were to do. Did you see this coming? God was leading us to believe for the purchase of that revolutionary building I mentioned earlier.

It even happened that following this revelation, the building just so happened to come up for sale within a few weeks. The area had begun to boom and was becoming a popular suburb within the growing inner city—perfect for a growing church.

Now, in the Baptist Church, any purchases or changes need a members' vote. So, this humble, Godly man, with the support of my parents, brought his written prophetic word to the members' meeting. This was the beginning of a very long and painful season for our family, for that man and his beautiful wife, and our church family. What had not been apparent for thirteen years of doing life with these people was that many of them were of the cessationist school of theology. In its most simplistic form, cessationism is the belief that spiritual gifts, including the gift of prophecy, came to an end with the death of the original apostles.

I know what you're thinking. How did you not know this before? As I mentioned, there weren't really any overt enough ways within our services or small groups for us to discover our differences. But they all came to the surface in that members' meeting, as people who that beautiful man had known since he was a boy accused him of being a false prophet. Subsequently, my parent's ability and authority to lead the church was also brought into question because of their belief that this was indeed a word from God.

Due to my age and stage of life, I had already begun wrestling with my faith, and sadly, I was quietly rebelling against God and my parents, so it was a very damaging time for this to occur. You see, I truly believed this was a word from God. Not just any word. A word He had also spoken to me as a young child who naively thought that God's word would excitedly and gratefully be received by our whole church family.

Unfortunately, a lot of people who, I guess, were just doing their best began to show a whole lot of fallen humanity to one another, and rather than just rejecting the word, people began to reject the messenger and his supporters.

Within six months, our church split, my parents were out of a job and my heart was broken, scared and angry. *If this is what hearing from God looks like, I don't want anything to do with it,* I thought. *And as for church… they can get stuffed. Is this how you treat people who have loved and served you for thirteen years?*

To make matters worse, within months, this man's wife (my mum's best friend) was diagnosed with a very aggressive form of cancer that took hold of her body so very quickly that she graduated to Heaven within twelve months. I have tears rolling down my face as I write this because for such a dignified, kind, loving and always gracious woman to have died still adjusting to the rejection and condemnation of lifelong friends, just seems too cruel for words. Of course, the accuser used people to declare that this was punishment for being a false prophet. I learned that prophecy was dangerous and that people were cruel and their love was conditional. I spiraled into full rebellion against God and church—a period that I would now call a deep, dark depression and return to my childhood anxiety. I didn't know which way was up anymore and I didn't care to try and figure it out.

My parents moved interstate, taking my two little sisters with them. I remained in Brisbane as I had just got engaged to my now husband, Jai. In what should have been one of the happiest seasons of my life, I struggled to understand God, the Holy Spirit, and what my purpose was. If this was church, I didn't want to know about it.

As I look back now, I am grateful that I found a way, with the help of the Holy Spirit, to forgive those who were good people and just defending what they feared but I also realise that the enemy was trying to steal, kill and destroy the very calling on my life—to be a prophet. I have to admit that my heart is in my mouth as I declare that this is who God has called me to be, but I have no reason to be ashamed or fearful about it.

This season culminated on my wedding day and the period of forced stillness during Chronic Fatigue. Ultimately my confusion and searching led me back to God in a more intimate way than before—because trying to live without Him and drowning out His voice during that time was painful and dark. It changed something in me that wasn't good. I sinned against God in my anger and disappointment in church and people in ways that I'm not proud of, and I had to seek forgiveness. I ran from God instead of running to Him. I wallowed in my pain and behaved in ways that weren't pretty. But here is the gift of that time: I cannot and will not live without His presence in my life for another day, *ever*—even if it means people misunderstand me or say unloving things about me. David's words became my testimony:

> Create in me a clean heart, O God, and renew a right spirit within me. Cast me not away from your presence, and take not your Holy Spirit from me. Restore to me the joy of your salvation, and uphold me with a willing spirit. (Psalm 51:10–12)

When David refers to his fear that the Holy Spirit would be taken from him because of his sin with

Bathsheba, which we read about in 2 Samuel 11, the Hebrew word he uses for Holy Spirit is *ruah*. It means 'breath' or 'wind'.[2] It was the *ruah* of God that created us and the world we live in,[3] and it was the *ruah* that led Ezekiel into the valley of dry bones that ultimately transformed the corpses into a vast army.[4] King David had seen first-hand what the Spirit of God departing from a man's life could look like. We have already talked about him administering musical medicine to King Saul once God's Spirit had departed from him. Saul became paranoid, delusional and egotistical once God's Spirit had left his life. But under the power of the Holy Spirit, Saul could prophesy and he became like another man[5]—in a good way! What an imprint this must have left on David's heart and life as he saw what a Spirit-filled life looked like—and a life devoid of the Spirit. This too is my testimony. I became paranoid, delusional, sick and broken when I rejected the Holy Spirit. But when filled with the Spirit of God, I am a better woman in every way.

In the New Testament Greek, this word *ruah* is translated *pneuma*—again meaning 'wind', 'breath' and 'spirit'.[6] This word is used 104 times in the Gospels, 72 times in the book of Acts, 146 times in Paul's letters, 37 times in the general letters and 26 times in Revelation. That's a total of 385 times in the New Testament.[7] This word is of huge importance not only in the Bible but in my own life as it is the prophetic naming of my church home—Neuma Church. Isn't it amazing that I came from a completely 'pneumaphobic'[8] environment to a church that is called Neuma Church because of its mandate to follow the leading of the Holy Spirit in making disciples across the nations? And the cherry on top—I now lead the prophetic pillar and spend my life training, empowering and releasing young and developing prophets in prayer, worship and ministry. Last laughs on you Satan!

As Dan McCollam says when speaking of his battle for the prophetic on his life, 'Conflict and criticism will either enlarge you or shrink you.'[9] I have chosen to grow into the fullness of my calling and I am on the lifelong journey of the fullness of maturity in Christ and the realm of the prophetic.

Through careful study of the Scriptures, a balanced reading of varying theological standpoints, and some very deep soul searching and healing, I believe that spiritual gifts are still very much on the menu right throughout God's Word and that worship devoid of the Holy Spirit can very easily become religious ritual. I don't claim to be superior to anyone who differs in theology, I just claim to have read in the pages of my Bible, seen with my eyes, and experienced in my heart too much in God to ever be able to doubt that He wants to move in and through us to heal, to prophesy and to operate in the fullness of the authority Jesus gave us.

I am also equally passionate about the Body of Christ being known for her love for one another and having the maturity to accept that there is unity in our diversity. I don't need everyone to be like me for me to love them and worship with them. There is too much that God has for us all to do for us to waste time on what we don't have in common. So please hear love and grace in this story—not fear or rejection.

When it comes to the biblical role of the *pneuma* of God in our worship—both personal and corporate—there are two stories, side by side in John's gospel, involving Jesus and a man named Nicodemus, and Jesus and a woman getting water at a well in Samaria. In these accounts, Jesus makes two statements about the *pneuma* that affect the way we worship today.

Nicodemus was a Pharisee, a ruler of the Jews and a member of the Sanhedrin who came to interview Jesus at night. Some scholars believe this was to avoid the crowds; others believe it was because he was seeking answers and hiding his belief in Jesus Christ from fellow Pharisees.[10] Either way, here we find Jesus teaching Nicodemus about spiritual birth. It all messes with Nico's noodle a little bit because it is like nothing he has ever read or heard of, nor does it seem possible in the natural.

> 'How can a man be born when he is old? Can he enter a second time into his mother's womb and be born?' Jesus answered, "Truly, truly, I say to you, unless one is born of the water and the Spirit [pneuma], he cannot enter the kingdom of God. That which is born of the flesh is flesh, and that which is born of the Spirit [pneuma] is spirit [pneuma]. Do not marvel that I said to you, 'You must be born again.' The wind [pneuma] blows where it wishes, and you hear its sound,

but you do not know where it comes from or where it goes. So it is with everyone who is born of the Spirit [pneuma]'" (John 3:4–8)

Notice that *pneuma* appears five times in these verses. There is so much theology in this little passage, but I want us to focus on that final verse—'The wind blows where it wishes, and you hear its sound, but you do not know where it comes from or where it goes. So it is with everyone who is born of the Spirit.' Theological commentators tell us that the wordplay contained here is difficult to explain adequately in English. But in its simplest form, it means something like this: the work of the Spirit is invisible and mysterious like the blowing of the wind.[11]

What Jesus was saying to Nicodemus, and what He is saying to us today, is that while we can all see the effects of the wind in both the natural and the spiritual realms, we cannot control it, nor should we seek to. This could have been either liberating or terrifying for Nicodemus. He was a man who taught the law, lived by the law and upheld the law. How do you contain the wind within the law? The answer is—you can't. This is why people often make the choice to stay within the comfort and safety of neat boxes and religious rules rather than getting out of the way to let the Spirit have His say.

Anyone who suffers from control issues will also struggle with the Spirit because He is not to be controlled. But here's the thing: you can't control the wind, but you can chase it, you can stand in it, and it can blow you clean and—you can even get swept up in it!

When I go for a run and the wind is in my face, it is struggle town! I remember one race I ran in on a cold Melbourne morning when I had the windy rain pummeling down into my face like sharp pins as I tried to make it around the dreaded Albert Park section of the annual City to Sea. I honestly didn't know if I could make it. I've run that track so many times, but this was so difficult because my body resisted the oncoming wind. It felt like my legs and my lungs were working doubly hard and I was running against a brick wall. But when I turned the corner towards the home stretch with the wind at my back, it was bliss! I ran more freely and lightly and I naturally gathered speed and momentum.

To resist the work of the Holy Spirit is to run against the wind of the Spirit rather than to run with it at your back, which gives you spiritual wings! Or maybe sails are a better metaphor. It's like we are the little sailboats, who, with humble trust and expectation, set our sails to the Holy Spirit wind and then our lives gather speed and momentum for the Kingdom. This is what grace should feel like—to follow God's calling into all He has for us and to feel the ease and joy of the journey as the *pneuma* carries us along. Being a wind chaser and getting carried along by His strength, wisdom and guidance is the adventure of a lifetime and it's completely safe because God is safe.

I had an encounter with the Lord during my January holiday this year. We head to the Sunshine Coast in sunny Queensland every year for a good dose of Vitamin D with the kids. It's such a sacred and special time for us. I always start the day having quiet time with God on our rooftop, where there is nothing between the ocean and me. I hear, see and experience God best when I'm in nature. I was contemplating what God would like me to focus on in the coming year. This is something I do each year to frame my year and to help build healthy boundaries and guidelines around what I will say yes and no to.

This particular morning as I asked God to show me what this year would hold, I lay back with my eyes closed and the sound of the ocean in the background, the sun warming my face and body, and I immediately entered a closed vision. In this vision, there was a leaf lying on a path. And there I was, in the middle of the path behind the leaf. Then, a light wind picked up and began to spin, lift and pinwheel the leaf down the path into the distance, and I began to chase after it. I was laughing and I was having an absolute ball chasing this leaf. Just as I would get close and reach out to catch it, the wind would pick up again, and off it would go… and the process repeated. The vision finished as quickly as it started and I knew what my assignment was for the year—follow the wind and take the time to enjoy the chase!

I've heard so many people express their fear that following the Holy Spirit can lead to weird places that don't reflect much biblical truth and even that being prophetic or Spirit-led is the market share of the spiritual lightweights or weirdos. This makes me so sad because these fears keep people resisting the wind rather than having it at their back. When Jesus talked about the kind of worship His Father was looking for, in His encounter with the woman at the well, He said this:

> 'But the hour is coming, and is now here, when the true worshipers will worship the Father in spirit [pneuma] and truth, for the Father is seeking such people to worship him. God is spirit [pneuma], and those who worship him must worship in spirit [pneuma] and truth.'
> (John 4:23–24)

There is so much rich, amazing contextual truth and application in this encounter Jesus had with this woman at the well but let's land on these two words— Spirit and truth. These are the two things the Father is seeking and actively looking for from His worshipers—a combination of *pneuma* and *aletheia*, which is the opposite of fictitious, feigned or false. In other words, not weird! Instead, it's Holy Spirit and it's real, sincere, accurate, truthful and dependable.[12]

One commentator explained that to worship in truth is worship that is doctrinally informed and directed towards Jesus; worship that affirms the realities of truth.[13] I understand that I am not adequately covering so much of the rich context and theology of this encounter here, but this is because I want you to hear this: prophetic worship that is Holy Spirit led does not have to be kooky! It can and should be completely grounded in Scripture, and therefore transformational.

Ephesians 6:17 calls the Word of God the 'sword of the Spirit' or 'sword of the *pneuma*'. When Paul says, 'the word of God' he uses the word *rhema*, which means the proclaimed or spoken Word of God.[14] So here we have again, the *pneuma* and the *rhema*. The Spirit and the Word. This combination becomes a weapon.

When we pick that sword up in worship through prayer, declaration and melody, we can literally slice through oppressive atmospheres and cut things off our lives that don't need to be there, and we do it all right alongside the Holy Spirit. We can also do some pretty decent damage to the kingdom of darkness.

I often tell our worship leaders that it is one thing to express your emotions to God in prayer or song, and this is a great and important thing to do, but if you want to do war with your worship—sing or pray Scripture. Emotions are like feather dusters that tickle other people's ears when we sing them. But singing Scripture is a sword that is an offensive weapon for God's Kingdom.

I absolutely love to chase the wind in my worship. Sometimes He moves fast. Sometimes He stays still— never stagnate, but still. Sometimes He will highlight a particular instrument when the musician is operating under the power of the Holy Spirit and it heals people— and just when we feel like we have a good handle on how it's all going to go, He takes off again and we start the pursuit all over again.

I also love to sing off the page in my worship. What do I mean by this? I leave behind the words of the songwriter and sing in my heavenly language. It's exactly what is described in Ephesians 5:18–19 when Paul instructs the church in Ephesus not to get drunk with wine, but be filled with the Spirit, addressing one another in psalms and hymns and spiritual songs, singing and making melody to the Lord with your heart. The thing about wine is that it influences the way we think and act. The *pneuma* of God does the same thing. It intoxicates us to the point where words of love and thanks pour out of us in a heavenly language.

Worship is *pneuma*. Let's chase the wind.

WORSHIP IS
Face to Face

We see God face to face every hour, and know the savor of Nature.

RALPH WALDO EMERSON[1]

When my husband and I got married two decades ago, we received one gift multiple times. As in four times! And it wasn't a platter or a kettle. It was a book, and chances are if you got married in the mid to late 90s, you could probably guess what book that was. It was, of course, the New York Times best-selling marriage book, *The 5 Love Languages*. This brilliant book outlines the five primary ways that we give and receive love based upon the way God individually wired us.

These five 'languages' include words of affirmation, acts of service, receiving gifts, quality time and physical touch.[2] For me, my love languages are words of affirmation, receiving gifts and quality time. And because opposites really do attract, you can probably guess what my husbands are. Yep—acts of service and physical touch.

Needless to say, after the initial honeymoon phase, the love was flowing and everything was unicorns and rainbows. It's amusing now as I look back, that God put that book into our hands four times over and yet we still never looked beyond the front cover until about ten years into our marriage. Like so many other couples, reading this book and coming to understand these love languages has changed our relationship in so many ways as we have learned how to serve each other and communicate love to each other more effectively.

As I mentioned, one of my love languages is quality time. What this means for me is that I love to have the people who make me feel safe in my presence. We don't necessarily have to be staring into one another's eyes and waxing lyrical about our love for one another; your mere presence will fill up my love tank.

Perhaps this is why I am pretty much obsessed with the Holy Spirit or *pneuma*, which we talked about in our last chapter. Now don't go getting all theologically bent out of shape—I'm not saying I have a favourite member of the Trinity or that one is more important than the other in our worship—so relax and stay with me. What I am saying is that because of the gift and the ministry of the Holy Spirit, I have before me an opportunity and an invitation for my quality time love tank to be constantly filled to overflowing.

In 1 Corinthians 3:16, we read, 'Do you not know that you are God's temple and that God's Spirit dwells in you?' Paul goes on to say in chapter 6 that 'your body is a temple of the Holy Spirit within you, whom you have from God' (1 Corinthians 6:19). Let me echo the Apostle Paul here and ask you, do you know that you are

God's temple and that His *pneuma* dwells within *you*? Probably the more important question is do you *live* like you know that God's Spirit dwells in you? When we live from this conviction and say a big 'yes' to God's invitation to have quality time and constant fellowship with the Holy Spirit, it changes the way we worship.

One of the approximate billion things I've learned in mothering my four incredible children is that the best gift I can give them—especially in those tender moments of doubt or when they lack confidence or perhaps seek wisdom—is to make eye contact with them as I speak into those painful, vulnerable and important parts of their little 'heart gardens'. I do this because my eye contact communicates more than my words do, and they know they have my undivided attention.

With the pace of life and the demands on family that we're all balancing, it can be easy to have important conversations over the phone, via text, or on the run, but to look my babies in the eye and to communicate with them heart to heart, is a gift of nurture that they need to thrive. Sometimes it's not even enough for me to just be in the same room as them; they need me to stop, lay aside everything else, stand face to face, eye to eye and let them feel seen and heard. As God's children, we are no different.

Did you know that our sensitivity to eye contact begins from when we are just two days old? Yes, you read that right—*two days old*. Studies have shown that infants at this early age and stage of life prefer looking into faces that lock eye contact with them. By four months of age, a baby's processing of people's faces is more deeply embedded when eye contact is made rather than when the gaze is averted.[3]

Do you know what this tells me? You and I are hardwired to want face-to-face interactions from birth, and the more we gaze into someone else's face, the more deeply embedded that person is in our brain and heart. Now I'm getting excited! Let's go on the journey together of discovering how this truth changes the way we worship.

There was a man in the Old Testament who lived this kind of intimate worship life with God. He is mentioned 767 throughout the pages of the Old Testament, and 79 times in the New Testament. I am, of course, speaking of Moses.

Moses' life was segmented into nice, neat forty-year seasons. He spent the first forty years of his life growing up in the house of Pharaoh learning the wisdom of Egyptians. His second forty years were lived as a fugitive from Pharaoh after killing an Egyptian for mistreating a Hebrew slave. At the age of eighty, he devoted the final forty years of his life to leading the Israelites out of slavery in Egypt and through four decades of wilderness wanderings.[4]

The pages of our Bible are full of the incredible encounters Moses had with God. The distinctive of his life and leadership was his pursuit and ability to host the presence of God. Moses' intimacy with God is inspiring in every way, and yet the Bible makes it clear that through the new covenant, we can experience greater intimacy than Moses. Don't rush past that. Take a moment here. The Bible makes it clear that through the new covenant, we can experience *greater* intimacy than Moses!

Deuteronomy 34:10 describes Moses as knowing the Lord 'face to face'. In Numbers 12:8 we read that God would speak to Moses 'mouth to mouth, clearly, and not in riddles'. Exodus 33:11 says, 'The LORD used to speak to Moses face to face, as a man speaks to his friend.'

In ancient Eastern culture, it was considered dishonourable to look a superior in the face, yet this wording is carefully chosen to paint the picture that Moses was conversing as an equal with God—not in stature, but relationally.[5] When Moses encountered God's face, it did not only affect him; it affected everybody around him.

In Exodus 34:29, we read that when Moses came out of his face-to-face encounter with God, 'Moses did not know that the skin of his face shone because he had been talking with God.' This word for 'shone' here means to be radiant, to have a shining appearance, to literally glow with supernatural beams of light.[6] Wait. What? Are you kidding? Moses spent so much time looking at the face of God, that his face began to reflect it… literally!

Moses' glow was so confronting that he had to sport a veil over his face so that his family and followers could cope with the effects of his face-to-face encounters with God. Moses would only remove this veil when he went into God's presence. This is a very significant metaphor and inclusion in God's Word for us as New Testament, new covenant believers. With this in mind, let's look at 2 Corinthians 3:7–9, 18.

> Now if the ministry of death, carved in letters on stone, came with such glory that the Israelites could not gaze at Moses' face because of its glory, which was being bought to an end, will not the ministry of the Spirit have even more glory? For if there was glory in the ministry of condemnation, the ministry of righteousness must far exceed it in glory.

> And we all, with unveiled face, beholding the glory of the Lord, are being transformed into the same image from one degree of glory to another. For this comes from the Lord who is the Spirit.

Let's look at a few of these words in the context and original language of this passage so that we can cop the full blow of the revelation that Paul is imparting here to the church in Corinth, and to us today. In verse 7 when he contrasts the law and the Spirit, Paul is referring to the fact that it was after receiving the Ten Commandments on Mount Sinai that Moses originally got his glow on. Paul poses the question then, if 'Mo can get his glow' while still subject to the law—which has now been made redundant by our once and for all sacrifice, Jesus—then how much more should we as new covenant, New Testament, *pneuma* filled believers be able to reflect God's glory?

We live in a time where we no longer have to sacrifice animals or fulfil the law to come close to God. We no longer require a priest to be our intermediary. Jesus made the sacrifice once and for all and became our Great High Priest, and then called us, His children, a royal priesthood that can minister to God in our personal worship lives. We have become ministers of the new covenant.[7] Each one of us!

When Paul then talks about us coming with 'unveiled faces', he is, of course, referencing the veil that Moses wore so that His intimacy with God was less of an affront to others.

How many times do we put masks on in our worship so that other people don't find our worship confronting? We have become quite good at knowing what is culturally appropriate in our churches and our worship services so that we walk that perfect tension of blending in, by being passionate enough to fit, and yet not so enamored that we would stand out. We have, in effect, put our veils back on before others and in the process, put a lid on our ability to reflect the glory of God to the world around us.

This reference to the veil gets even cooler when we think of it in the context of what happened at that moment when Jesus hung on a cross, absorbed our sin on His perfect body, and became the payment for our intimacy with the Father.

In Matthew 27:50–51, we read, 'And Jesus cried out again with a loud voice and yielded up his spirit. And behold, the curtain of the temple was torn in two, from top to bottom.' Imagine that with me for a moment.

What would it have been like for those in the temple at the time when this thick, heavy and bulky, sacred curtain was supernaturally torn from top to bottom? It would have been noisy, dramatic and epic! In fact, according to Jewish tradition, the Priests who were in the temple at that time did not understand what happened, and they attempted to sew the curtain back up!

This curtain was also referred to as 'the veil of the temple'. Absorb the significance of this. The ark, which was symbolic of the glory of the Lord that was kept behind this now torn veil, this same glory that was reflected on Moses' face, was now unveiled once and for all as Jesus' spirit left the earth and the sacrifice was made. Access was now gained for every one of us, under the new covenant, to come into an intimate relationship with Him, never having to wear a veil or a mask again. No longer living in His proximity, but invited into intimacy.

I love how Brian Simmonds describes this new intimacy in Hebrews 4:16: 'So now we come freely and boldly to where love is enthroned, to receive mercy's kiss and discover the grace we urgently need to strengthen us in our time of weakness' (TPT). This is exactly what it means to worship God with an unveiled face. It's the freedom and confidence to worship God face to face that comes from knowing everything has been done to conquer our fear, shame and sin.

I have found that one of the ways I know my kids are carrying guilt and shame in their hearts is when they avoid making eye contact with their father or me. It's a dead giveaway, but don't tell them that. They avert their gaze. They look at anything but into my eyes and I know straight away—guilty!

In my own life, this is often what keeps me in the zone of proximity and out of the place of face-to-face intimacy with Jesus. We carry guilt and shame that Jesus has already paid for, and the enemy wins the war for our worship and renders us ineffective for the Kingdom by keeping our eyes on things other than our Champion. You see, as long as we've got our eyes on our sin and shame, we are not looking to Jesus. And if we're not looking to Jesus, we cannot become more like Him. Here's the thing: if we want to *become*, we have to *behold*.

The word 'beholding' in 2 Corinthians 3:18 means to 'reflect'. Reflect what? God's glory. God's *doxa*. His splendour. His brightness. His shining radiance. A mirror can only reflect what looks into it. That's profound, I know, but think about it for a moment. As we make face-to-face, eye-to-eye contact with glory, we soon reflect His glory on our faces and in our hearts, and we are transformed into His likeness just like a mirror.

We will talk more about this mirror concept in Chapter 9, but let me remind you here of one of our New Testament biblical words from our introduction to describe worship. The word *doxazo* means to glorify God in word or deed.[8] Our lives become our worship when we model our lives on the life of Jesus. This is *doxazo*. And this kind of worship leads to transformation. Again, we become like what we behold.

To be 'transformed' means to be completely made into something else. The original word is the word *metamorphoo*, from which we take our word metamorphosis. Most of us would be familiar with this word from our primary school years when we learn about the transformation of a caterpillar into a butterfly.[9] This is what Paul is saying happens to us. We change in both appearance and essential nature until we reflect the image of God himself to the world around us.

Even more remarkable is that Paul says we are being 'transformed into the same *eikon*',[10] using a word that carries the same meaning as the Hebrew word, *selem*, found in Genesis 1:27: 'So God made man in his own image, in the image of God he created him; male and female he created them.' We'll talk about this more in a later chapter, but for now, catch that!

As we worship God, as we remove our masks and veils and come freely and confidently, as we behold His glory, we are transformed into His likeness and back into our Eden state. In other words, we bring Kingdom to earth in our lives. But this only happens when we choose to lay aside our veils of guilt, condemnation and shame, and worship face to face.

Moses was a man who was the exception to Old Testament culture. He encountered God face to face and was known as a friend of God. Hebrews 12:1–2 is one of my favourite Scriptures in the whole Bible because it is one of the New Testament framings or calls to live the way Moses did: 'And let us run with perseverance the race marked out for us, fixing our eyes on Jesus, the pioneer and perfecter of faith.'

To run our race well, we need to not be looking to the left or the right. If we choose to behold others more than we behold God, we will soon be transformed into their image. We all know about the pitfalls of the comparison trap, but I dare say that at times the Church has fallen into this.

In our desire to serve the world well, we have, at times, spent more time looking at the world's culture and methods than we have asking God what He thinks and wants to say about things, and soon we reflect the culture more than we reflect Kingdom. This can happen in our worship too, but I believe that we are in a season where God is restoring His vision for the Church and worship to His chosen leaders, and there is a restoration of sorts to the original blueprint taking place. To see this fulfilled, we will need to fix our eyes on Jesus, and in doing so, we are metamorphosed into our Eden selves and into the Church that exists in God's heart.

We can worship our way to restoration. We can only do this if we choose to take our eyes off others, remove our masks and step boldly into face-to-face encounters with God. The really good news is this: none of this is produced 'by might, nor by power, but by my Spirit, says the LORD of hosts' (Zechariah 4:6).

We will never *bear* God's image if we don't first *behold* God's image. We will never carry God's glory if we don't first worship God's glory. We will never bring

Kingdom to earth if we don't first catch a glimpse of what His Kingdom looks, sounds, tastes and smells like. We find these things, not in the proximity of Jesus, but as we come face to face with Him—as we behold Him in all of His love, His beauty, His wisdom and His might. And the more time we spend beholding, the more of our lives we will live becoming!

Worship is face to face, and under the new covenant, this invitation isn't for the one in a million, it's for each of us—yes, YOU! Brian Simmonds translates 2 Corinthians 3:18 this way:

> We can all draw close to him with the veil removed from our faces. And with no veil we all become like mirrors who brightly reflect the glory of the Lord Jesus. We are being transfigured into his very image as we move from one brighter level of glory to another. And this glorious transfiguration comes from the Lord, who is the Spirit. (TPT)

Worship is face to face. Let's remove the veils and come close.

WORSHIP IS
Shoulder to Shoulder

One hundred religious persons knit into a unity by careful organization do not constitute a church any more than eleven dead men make a football team.

A.W. TOZER[1]

I am in one of the most unique seasons of my entire life. I've certainly never faced a season like this before, and I hope I don't ever have to again. I'm writing this chapter enshrouded in 'COVID-19 Stage 4 lockdown' in dark, cold, moody, wintery Melbourne, Australia. It's been thirty weeks since I've had 'smashed avo' on toast with a long black or almond latte at my favourite café. If you're a Melbournian like me, you know this is true suffering and not normal Melbournian behaviour!

But more importantly, it's been thirty Sundays or nearly seven long months since I have been a part of corporate worship. This is the longest time in my whole life that I have not stood *shoulder to shoulder* with my church family and lifted a unified love song to our Saviour. And it hurts. I miss it. I miss the people. I miss the community. I miss my favourite sound in the whole world… the sound of the Bride of Christ confessing her love, hope, theology and belief in God. Even when I ran from God for a season, somehow, I just couldn't stay away from corporate worship. No matter what activity I'd try to fill my Sundays with as I ran in anger from the Church, I'd still inexplicably find myself sneaking in up the back just to get a dose of corporate worship.

In my local church, we've done our best to serve people well in this season. We've done church online and engaged in loving people in the most creative and connected (but distanced) ways we could prayerfully imagine. And God is definitely doing some significant sifting in His Church that I'm aware of and grateful for, but I just can't wait to worship with my covenant family again.

When we say the word 'church' it conjures up so many different images for so many people. Some people cringe at the concept of a church, believing it to be a crusty, outdated and irrelevant institution with nothing to offer their modern lives. Other people feel a pang of pain in their hearts because they were once vulnerable enough to stand shoulder to shoulder with people from different backgrounds and cultures to try to build trust-based relationships, and sadly they got hurt or disappointed. Other people immediately think of the place that they are obligated to attend out of a sense of duty once a week or perhaps at Christmas and Easter time.

And then there are those, like me, whose hearts beat a little bit faster at the mention of the Church. Have I been hurt in church? Of course, I have. But I have had to choose not to let my experience of people's best efforts to be and to build the Church determine my theology of what is in God's heart for the Church as is clearly laid out in His Word for us.

By now, you know that I'm all about those face-to-face encounters that we can individually have and are invited into, just like Moses was. But a well-rounded worship life that leads to a holistically healthy life includes both the individual face-to-face encounters as well as the corporate, shoulder-to-shoulder experience. In Psalm 92:12-15, we read this about people who worship shoulder to shoulder with the Body of Christ:

> The righteous flourish like the palm tree and grow like a cedar in Lebanon. They are planted in the house of the LORD; they flourish in the courts of our God. They still bear fruit in old age; they are ever full of sap and green, to declare that the LORD is upright; he is my rock, and there is no unrighteousness in him.

Did you catch that? We flourish when we worship shoulder to shoulder with the church family we are planted in. In fact, our personal face-to-face worship lives and our corporate shoulder-to-shoulder worship experiences are perhaps more connected than one might first think.

We are wired to desire the sense of belonging found in relational communities or families. Our world craves it, and so do we. Even our triune God is relational by very nature. People are looking and searching for belonging, sometimes in all the wrong places. God made us this way and the search is meant to lead us to our only true home—relationship with Jesus, which is then watered and protected in the House of God. I believe the sense of belonging we all so deeply desire can only truly be found in its intended fullness and richness within the Body of Christ. King David was a man who discovered what is intended for all of us in God's House. Meditate for a moment on his words and ask yourself if this is the way you think about the Church:

> Here's the one thing I crave from God, the one thing I seek above all else: I want the privilege of living with him every moment in his house, finding the sweet loveliness of his face, filled with awe, delighting in his glory and grace. I want to live my life so close to him that he takes pleasure in my every prayer. In his shelter in the day of trouble, that's where you'll find me, for he hides me there in his holiness. He has smuggled me into his secret place, where I'm kept safe and secure… (Psalm 27:4–7 TPT)

Is this your confession about the Church? It's okay if it's not, but can I encourage you? Dig a little bit deeper. Because if it isn't, perhaps your love, or lack therefore for the Church, is predominantly based on your experience, rather than on the Church that exists in God's heart that is revealed to us through His Word. This may even be a key indicator as to why worshiping shoulder to shoulder is not easy or fulfilling for you.

Perhaps in corporate worship, you feel like a spectator? Let's go there!

Whenever I notice my sense of passion waning for the corporate, shoulder-to-shoulder experience, I find it helpful to examine God's Word once again for the reality of the vision He has for the Church and to let that become the barometer for my expectation. In other words, I choose not to let my disappointment level taint my faith or inform my theology. This would shrink my world down drastically and it would also diminish my ability to experience the fullness that Jesus died to offer me. It could also decrease my connection and contribution to the thing that He is returning for—His Church.

As we have seen, David discovered that the Church in God's heart offers us a sense of belonging and wholeness in our hearts, minds *and* souls. While we can engage our physical bodies and thoughts in other places of belonging such as sporting clubs, nightclubs, and even religious clubs, they can often be seditiously damaging to the condition and health of our souls; ultimately increasing the void that can only be fulfilled in a loving relationship with Jesus, 'the head of the body, the church' (Colossians 1:18).

It is Paul, in 1 Corinthians 12:27, who uses the metaphor of the physical body to describe this community of belonging that we call the Church. He writes, 'You are the body of the Anointed One, and each of you is a unique and vital part of it' (TPT). Eugene Peterson paraphrases verses 25–26 this way:

The way God designed our bodies is a model for

understanding our lives together as a church: every part dependent on every other part, the parts we mention and the parts we don't, the parts we see and the parts we don't. If one part hurts, every other part is involved in the hurt, and in the healing. If one part flourishes, every other part enters into the exuberance. (MSG)

Paul penned this letter in response to a very specific issue that had begun to appear within the community of believers in Corinth. Some members of the newly formed church were able to speak in tongues, and others could not. The ones who could, believed that this was a sign of their spiritual superiority and that *glossolalia* was a superior gift rendering the other spiritual gifts of lesser importance—and you thought it was just your church or life group that struggled with the tongues issue!

This is where the Holy Spirit's revelation of the Church as a body was helpful to the church in Corinth and is helpful for wherever our churches are today. Paul speaks of a body where every part is dependent on the other, well connected and in unity and harmony where if one part flourishes, the rest rejoice. In reality, the very gifts that God gave this local body in Corinth to build them up and strengthen them were causing division and derision. How often do we see this in the Church today? Rather than celebrating and honouring one another's gifts that come from Heaven, we develop classes and echelons of importance that don't reflect what is in God's heart for His Church at all.

Chances are, the issues you deal with in your church community today have been an issue at one point or another in church history. Perhaps even at the birth of the early church like we see here, the issues you face today could be affecting your desire to worship shoulder to shoulder. Even if the particular circumstances are not exactly the same, they're probably very similar and could very well come from the same root cause because people are people, and the church is made up of... you guessed it—people. We are the Church! Paul puts it this way in 1 Corinthians 3:16–17: 'Do you not know that you are God's temple and that God's Spirit dwells in you? If anyone destroys God's temple, God will destroy him. For God's temple is holy, and you are that temple.' Them fighting words Pauly!

It is not the unicorns and rainbows part of church life that Paul is addressing in the passage about the body, but the differences and the tensions. He is teaching that we don't all have to agree on every single thing to be able to be unified, but that there can be unity in our diversity when our foundation is love. Just because we disagree, doesn't mean we should stand back to back rather than shoulder to shoulder. It is very difficult to take ground in invading the earth with God's Kingdom if we are facing away from one another rather than choosing to remain shoulder to shoulder. Likewise, as he says in 1 Corinthians, it is serious business to turn away from one another and destroy God's temple with our words and withdrawals over our disagreements.

This is why I love that Jesus Christ is described as the 'head' of the body. Think about what is positioned *on* or *in* your head: your brain or your ability to think, your eyes that provide you with vision, your ears that enable you to hear, your nose that gives you smell, and your mouth and tongue, which you speak from and taste with. The only sensory function that is not positioned primarily on your head is your ability to touch.

Could it be that the headship of Jesus Christ metaphor exists to teach us that it will only be when the Church thinks, sees, hears, smells, and speaks as Jesus does, that we will be ready for him to '...present the church to himself in splendor, without spot or wrinkle or any such thing, that she might be holy and without blemish' (Ephesians 5:27)?

Maybe it is only then that we will be ready for what John saw in his spirit when he wrote, 'for the marriage of the Lamb has come, and his Bride has made herself ready; it was granted her to clothe herself with fine linen, bright and pure' (Revelation 19:7–8). And maybe it's only when we live in this revelation and reality that we are ready to reach out and touch the world outside of our four walls and represent Christ well.

In the same way that Jesus didn't do or say anything He didn't see His Father doing,[2] the Church is the fulfilment of what is in God's heart when we do the same. We not only have His thoughts, but we can think like He thinks because 'we have the mind of Christ' (1 Corinthians 2:16). We can see things the way God sees and have the 'Spirit of wisdom and of revelation in the knowledge of him, having the eyes of your hearts enlightened' (Ephesians 1:17-18). From this place of having His thoughts and seeing what He sees, we can then speak what He would speak. Jesus himself taught His disciples that 'the Holy Spirit will teach you in that very hour what you ought to say' (Luke 12:12).

How can the Church smell like Christ? We read in 2 Corinthians 2:14–15, 'But thanks be to God, who in Christ always leads us in triumphal procession, and through us spreads the fragrance of the knowledge of him everywhere. For we are the aroma of Christ…' As we spread the Gospel to our family and friends, as we preach the Gospel in our services and as we share our testimonies, we spread the fragrance of Christ everywhere and these words have an aroma. And when we hear what Jesus hears or tune into the frequency of Heaven, we align all of our senses with the headship of Christ Jesus, making us ready for the ultimate marriage celebration.

In John 10:27, Jesus tells us, 'My sheep hear my voice, and I know them, and they follow me.' Every child of God has an inheritance—the ability to hear Jesus' voice and to follow it. The way we access His voice is by 'knowing' Him.

I love to think of it this way: when my husband sends me a text message, the internal voice I read it in is not my voice, but his. I hear the words he emphasizes, and how his intonation sounds. This is because I know him. I have known the man for over twenty years, and we are in constant communication and have made the decision to spend the rest of our lives continuing to build our friendship through communication. However, if someone I have never met sends me a text message, the internal voice I hear is my own voice. This is because I don't know what they sound like yet. The more I get to know that person, the more likely that I will soon hear their written words in their audible voice internally.

The same is true of our relationship with God. The more time we spend getting to know Him through the reading of the Word and time spent in intimate connection, the more likely we are to hear His voice internally in ways that fully reflect His character. If you want to know how to better hear His voice, get to know Him through His Word and through time in His presence.

As the Body of Christ, with Jesus as the head, we have been given the ability with the help of the Holy Spirit, to represent Him in His fullness. We do this best when we accept His invitation to think how He thinks, carry His vision for the earth and lay down our will and agenda. When we say what He would lovingly say about the issues our society faces, we spread the fragrance of Christ everywhere that His voice leads. This is the mandate of the Church! And the awesome thing about Him being the head is that we don't have to fight or dismember ourselves from the Body over what we think we should do, say, or where we should go because we are not the head. We find biblical unity when we unite around learning to hear and see what God says and sees for the Church in any given season.

I could go off on a whole tangent here about the Apostles and the Prophets seeing and hearing for the Church according to Ephesians 4 and how biblically it is the five-fold leadership structure in a church who represent this fragrance, but that's a whole other book so maybe stay tuned. For now, you get the picture. We are united, under the headship of Jesus Christ, and all that entails. Let's not be disunified by all trying to be the head. That's just weird. And you know what they say about people with two heads? Never good things!

We have touched on another of the metaphors used to describe the Church—a Bride. In Ephesians, the Church and Jesus Christ are compared to a husband and wife. We are taught that the way a man loves his wife should be a reflection of how Jesus, the Bridegroom, loves the Church.

I remember the day I got married. I was twenty years old and I knew nothing. Funnily enough, I thought I knew everything. I was riddled with insecurity and was immature in my understanding of my identity in Christ. So much so that even though I arrived at the church, accompanied by my dad in a luxurious limo and clad in a gorgeous, billowing silk gown, I did not want to get out of the car. When my dad asked me why I wouldn't move, I shared with him that all of a sudden, I was crippled by the realisation that while I walked down the aisle, people were going to look at me.

In my insecurity, this was the worst thing that could happen to me—having 120 sets of eyes boring holes in my fragile spirit. I was dressed the part of the spotless and ready bride, but internally, I was far from walking in this identity.

Sometimes I think this is an appropriate reflection of what the Church has become. We live in times where there are many contentious issues that we are afraid to speak up about because we're not sure that we are *grounded* enough in love to *respond* in love under pressure. We worry about how we will be perceived and what people will think about us. But it is time for the Bride of Christ to rediscover who she is and to speak with confidence the thoughts and visions about the realities of the Kingdom that God has revealed to her, and then leave the outcomes to God. But of course, if we don't speak in love, even the most profound truths from God's heart will be nothing but a 'noisy gong or a clanging cymbal' (1 Corinthians 13:1).

I am the proud mother of three boys, and finally, I got my girl. All my kids are about two years apart, so when little Miss Eden Isabel came into the world, she had three big brothers: two, four and six-years-old. Because I was so excited to be having a princess, I created a 'Kingdom of Pinkdom'. I filled her little room with trinkets, dolls and frills. I was so excited to exchange Tonka Trucks for tea parties! The problem was, the boys loved to visit Pinkdom and 'hybrid' her dolls. They would take their Spiderman head and put it on an innocent baby doll creating 'Spiderbaby'. Sometimes, I would find limbs strewn across Pinkdom, much to my horror! Essentially, my boys had created a crime scene out of the sanctuary I had set aside to be the land of Princess dreams.

In 1 Corinthians 12:18, we read, 'But as it is, God arranged the members in the body, each one of them as he chose.' If you have followed the voice of God to a local church body and you have left because of hurt and disappointment, we take what is meant to represent a functioning and effective body, and we turn it into a crime scene. If God arranged you in the Body, it follows that it is only He who can 'un-arrange' you. (I just made up a word but don't get distracted.) It is kind of like amputating ourselves for no good reason.

Having a limb amputated is known to be one of the most painful physical things that the human body can ever endure, let alone the emotional and spiritual effects. In Australia alone, there are over 8,000 lower limb amputations per year.[3] Often associated with these amputations is a syndrome called 'Phantom Limb Pain' which was discovered by Ambrose Pare, a sixteenth-century French military surgeon.[4] This is where painful sensations that seem to be coming from the amputated limb are experienced until the brain adjusts to the lack of signalling being sent from the affected limb.[5] In some cases, patients report phantom limb pain for up to fifty years after they lose their limb.[6]

Let's draw a spiritual parallel. When we 'amputate' ourselves from the Body over hurt and disappointment, when we turn away from the shoulder-to-shoulder worship, the rest of the Body will experience the pain of that separation. Paul puts it this way: 'If one member suffers, all suffer together' (1 Corinthians 12:26). God's vision for His Church is one of unity. In Psalm 133:1–3, we read the following:

> Behold, how good and pleasant it is when brothers dwell in unity! It is like the precious oil on the head, running down on the beard, on the beard of Aaron, running down on the collar of his robes! It is like the dew of Hermon, which falls on the mountains of Zion! For there the LORD has commanded the blessing, life forevermore.

This little Psalm is remarkable because once again, it presents the Church as having a sound and a fragrance. The context of this Psalm is that the people of Israel would travel to Jerusalem for their Jewish festivals and sing this 'song of ascent' as they literally ascended the hill to the temple, shoulder to shoulder.[7] As the various tribes and families gathered—men, women and children of all ages from different geographic locations—they were unified in one song, with one voice, and the sound could be heard for miles. Their unity, amidst their diversity, had a melodic, harmonious sound. Not only this, but David compared this unity to the anointing oil that was used to anoint the priest, Aaron. This oil was highly fragrant, holy and sacred, and mixed exclusively for anointing priests.[8] As the priest was anointed, it omitted a fragrance that people could smell from some distance.

This Psalm paints the picture that not only does unity have a melodic and harmonious sound—it is fragrant. The symbolism of this oil being poured on the head could be symbolic of Jesus Christ as the head of the Church. As it flows down the beard, shoulders, and onto the breastplate, which was inscribed with the names of all the twelve tribes of Israel, it is a beautiful picture of the anointing of Jesus Christ that we receive as part of His body.[9] We carry His sound and His fragrance, but only as we worship shoulder to shoulder, just like our spiritual forefathers did. And there we receive His blessing symbolised by the 'dew of Hermon' that speaks of God's blessing and provision for us, His children.[10]

You see, when we worship face to face in the secret place, we create an individual stream. Then when we come together shoulder to shoulder, each of our collective streams joins together and creates a raging river that can fill the House. But, wait—there's more. This river does not just fill the House but flows out the doors and into our communities, just as Ezekiel envisioned.[11] Ezekiel describes water flowing out of the temple like a river of life flowing out into the wilderness and turning these arid spaces into luscious gardens that bear fruit.[12]

This is what our collective worship can do. It can become a river where '...everything will live where the river goes' (Ezekiel 47:9). The problem is that this cannot happen if we do not come together and join our streams. There is something beautiful about cultivating the purity of your own stream, and you know by now—I'm all about it! But to be truly effective for the Kingdom in our world, we have to come together as the Body, join our streams, and then we can have a greater impact for God than any one individual could.

Has the Church made mistakes? Yes. Has the Church hurt good people? Undoubtedly. Is the Church perfect? No. All that says to me is that God is not finished yet. One of my core values is to take God at His Word and to keep it simple—endeavouring not to overcomplicate it.

When Jesus said in Matthew 16:18, 'I will build my church, and the gates of hell shall not prevail against it', I believe Him. When the Apostle Paul articulated his revelation in Ephesians 5:25–27 that Christ 'gave himself up' for His Bride and that He would cleanse her by the 'washing of water with the word, so that he might present the church to himself in splendor, without spot or wrinkle', I believe him. Not only do I believe him, but I also choose to give my life to co-labour with Jesus to bring His Kingdom to earth. I can do this by learning to think, talk, and hear as Jesus did. As I do this, I carry His fragrance and His sound to a world that needs Him. This is my worship—to carry the fragrance of Christ alongside my brothers and sisters, shoulder to shoulder.

When each of us individually owns our space and responsibility to do this, then when we come together and worship shoulder to shoulder, we bring a magnified, harmonious, symphonic and fragrant piece of Heaven to earth. We become a representation of what John saw in a vision: 'After this I looked, and behold, right in front of me I saw a vast multitude of people—an enormous multitude so huge that no one could count—made up of victorious ones from every nation, tribe, people group, and language' (Revelation 7:9 TPT).

Where else on earth could you find such a diverse group of people from every nation, tribe and tongue but the Church? And when we stand shoulder to shoulder, and we lift our worship to our God, we become a Kingdom manifestation. We become Kingdom on earth. Shoulder to shoulder.

WORSHIP IS
Hide and Seek

Without solitude it is virtually impossible to live a spiritual life.

HENRI NOUWEN[1]

When my kids were little, they loved to play hide and seek, on the daily. The interesting thing was I could learn a lot about their little personalities by how they approached playing this game. Have you noticed that? You can learn *a lot* about people by playing games with them. When it came to my four kids, I discovered a lot about their age and stage of life, and even their brain's developmental maturity.

When Eden was just one, River was three, Cabe was five and Noah was six, this game was particularly intriguing to observe. Eden would plonk herself down in the middle of the room, cover her eyes and think she was invisible. Not only was she completely visible, but she would proceed to yell out, 'I'm over here... I'm over here!' Eden's hide and seek approach was more like a moment of show and tell, which was a sign of her age and maturity at the time. We could see her and hear her, but she was sure she was the boss of this game.

Cabe, whose one sole purpose in life is to never, ever, ever, ever be still, wasn't a huge fan of this game. He couldn't think of anything worse than finding a dark corner to hide in and remaining completely still until someone found him! Not only was this game like admitting defeat to him, but it also felt like torture because he had to be still. His competitive nature would not allow him to make his hiding place as obvious as Eden, but it would only ever be a five-minute game with Cabe as he could endure stillness no longer and would soon reveal himself to the seeker. His personality is much more suited to show and tell than hide and seek.

Noah, my eldest—pragmatic, sensible, measured, intelligent, thoughtful firstborn, couldn't seem to accept this game as logical or necessary. He lives by Einstein and Jobs' lifestyle philosophy of making minimal small life choices to allow all of your thinking to be used on decisions that really matter in life.

Einstein is reported to have worn the same thing every single day because he didn't want to waste brainpower on choosing an outfit each morning. Steve Jobs had a similar life philosophy, and so does Noah. So you can see that spending valuable brainpower on coming up with new hiding places was superfluous and wasteful to my guy. His strategy was to come up with two moderately successful hiding places that he would use every single time we played the game. You knew you were either going to find him in our walk-in wardrobe or under his bed. He never deviated from this plan just like Steve Jobs never deviated from his plan while standing in his closet every morning! This meant that he complied with our request to be part of the family game quickly so he could tick it off the list and get on with more important things in life, like designing Lego planets or launching rockets off the back trampoline to the moon.

Now let's talk about River. I've left him until last because he is a ninja at hide and seek. I'm talking beast mode here. He will probably publish a book one day on how to play the game for the rest of us rookies that need his secrets. River would pack a backpack in preparation for the daily game. He would pack the same amount of supplies that I would pack for our entire family to go on a camping trip to the bush for a week. (Not that I go camping, but if I did, this is what I imagine I would pack). He packed snacks, a water bottle, games, books, toys, a change of clothes and a blankie. River has a tiny little frame, so he could hide in impossible places, remain completely silent, and enjoy his personal space and world for hours on end.

Hide and seek really is an introvert's dream. In fact, he stayed hidden for so long one day that we didn't realise he was still playing until he was missing from the dinner table *four* hours later. He was deliriously happy in his little cave, hidden away under the bottom shelf of the kitchen pantry. He even asked if he could finish his picture encyclopedia on the animal kingdom before coming to dinner!

The Bible talks about a different type of hide and seek. In the same way that each of my children's personalities, ages and stages of development and maturity affects how they play hide and seek, it also affects how willing and available we are to hide away and seek God's face. Let's go there together in Matthew 6:5-8:

> 'And when you pray, you must not be like the hypocrites. For they love to stand and pray in the synagogues and at the street corners, that they may be seen by others. Truly, I say to you, they have received their reward. But when you pray, go into your room and shut the door and pray to your Father who is in secret. And your Father who sees in secret will reward you.
>
> And when you pray, do not heap up empty phrases as the Gentiles do, for they think that they will be heard for their many words. Do not be like them, for your Father knows what you need before you ask him.'

To give some context to what Jesus was addressing in this passage, He was speaking particularly to the Pharisees and their propensity to approach their prayer and worship lives like it was show and tell, rather than hide and seek. The Father's intention for us is that like Jesus, all of our lives would flow from our hide and seek worship lives. As we discussed in our biblical definitions of worship, *sebo* was worship to any god in Greco Roman culture that focused on the external performance to gain favour.[2] In other words, show and tell worship lives. As you know by now, worship is so much more than the songs that we sing. Our worship lives are our whole lives, and Romans 12 makes this very clear. Worship is focusing on the daily disciplines that eventually become a delight, including prayer and the reading of God's Word.

This word 'hypocrites' or *hypokrites* which we find in verse five, is an important word in this passage. It literally means an actor, pretender, an insincere person or someone who is duplicitous.[3] It speaks of the actors in ancient Rome who would put masks on their faces and speak from underneath that mask.

Eventually, this word became culturally common to describe people who wore 'masks' and pretended to be someone or something other than their authentic selves. In using this word throughout Matthew 6, Jesus was comparing the religious worship practices of giving, prayer and fasting to the role-play of these actors. This was worship that had become about self and others, not God. It had become *sebo*—show and tell.

Not only were they pretending to be someone other than themselves before God, but they were making sure they were in the most public of places when they did it. Jews would traditionally pray and worship at least three times a day—morning, afternoon and evening. They would either pray in the temple, or just stop wherever they were at the set time of prayer, and pray.

What piqued Jesus' interest was that many Pharisees 'just so happened' to be on the busiest street corners at the time of prayer to ensure they had the maximum audience size. Sounds a lot like show and tell! It drives home the point for you and me that when it comes to our worship, we can do all the right things for all the wrong reasons and it won't impress God. We can appear to be serving God, but actually be serving ourselves. Ouch! How do we avoid this? By spending more time hiding away and seeking God's face than we do chasing the show and tell moments of life. Jesus' answer was not to stop worshiping but to teach us to focus on where, how and why we worship.

It's worth noting here that verse four, five and six, all start with the same theme—when... you... pray. We see here that Jesus assumes that our hide and seek worship lives will include regular, devoted, effective private prayer lives. We human beings are wired to pray and wired to want to connect with a higher being, and it's not just Christians who pray.

Timothy Keller explains that in all of 'the great monotheistic religions of Islam, Judaism, and Christianity, prayer is at the very heart of what it means to believe'.[4] It is not limited to these traditions, though. Buddhists also pray, as do Hindus. Australia's Indigenous people believe in multiple deities that they connect with in spiritual practices that include prayer.[5] This is because every single human being is wired to want to pray.

A recent study showed that one in five adults admitted praying, despite also identifying as 'non-religious'.[6] Interestingly, during the COVID-19 crisis, 28 percent of surveyed Australians, both non-religious and religious, admitted that they were praying more.[7] Again, this is because humans have been created to desire communication with divinity.

It's funny how in times of crisis or stress, we seem to instinctively know how to cry out to God for His help, whether we acknowledge Him as Lord or not. My father is a great example of this. He was not raised in a Christian family and would admit that he was actively running from God in many ways. I am the third of five children and the night of my birth was not simple.

My mother had been labouring for twenty-seven hours when the doctors approached my dad and gave him the news that probably no father ever wants to hear—'You have to choose. We can either save your wife or your baby.' It was at this moment that my dad prayed a prayer to a God that he didn't serve that went something like this: 'God, if you are real, save both my wife and my baby and I will serve you for the rest of my life.'

Fifteen minutes later, I came into the world (still inside the amniotic sac) with a big bang and a whole lot of noise and I'm proud to say I have been making a whole lot of noise ever since. In response, my dad gave his heart to God and vowed to serve Him for the rest of his life. He later went to Bible College and pastored in the Baptist Church for the decades that followed, and still does to this day.

In a beautiful moment of divine orchestration, my dad named me 'Stacey Renee' because he just 'liked' those names. He had no idea what these names meant, much to my mum's disgust. She too was overwhelmed at the bigness and yet the intricacy of God when she discovered that Stacey means 'resurrection' while Renee means 'reborn'.[8]

On the night of my natural birth, my dad came into spiritual rebirth and named his newborn daughter 'resurrection... reborn'. Only God! My dad found out first hand that night that God is not too religious to answer the prayers of people who don't even know if He's real. I would go as far as to say that He delights in answering the prayers of those who long to know if He exists and that He loves proving Himself to be faithful in pursuing the lost and hearing their cries. He is, after all, the Shepherd who leaves the ninety-nine to go after the one.[9]

The great Martin Luther is known to have said this: 'As it is the business of tailors to mend clothes and cobblers to make shoes, so it is the business of Christians to pray.'[10] We are wired for connection with our Heavenly Father, and this connection is fostered when we worship and pray.

I have found that worship and prayer are inseparable, both in experience and biblically. It would be like trying to have a wedding with just a bride or just a groom. It's just not possible—you need both. In the same way, Scripture majors on both worship and prayer as foundational elements in the early Church and in individual relationship and intimacy with Jesus. One simply cannot be living a life of worship and not be prioritising time in prayer. Likewise, we can't spend time in effective prayer and it not become an expression of heartfelt worship. They are simply inseparable, and it is non-biblical to seek to separate them.

Romans 12:1–2 (MSG) teaches us that our worship lives are our 'everyday, ordinary' lives—our 'sleeping, eating, going-to-work, and walking-around' lives placed before God as an offering of worship.

Paul tells us in 1 Thessalonians 5:17 to 'pray without ceasing' or to pray continuously. We are meant to be in constant communication and connection with God. This is a life lived in worship. This is a life that understands that the show and tell part of our worship lives are nothing but hypocrisy if not an overflow of our hide and seek lives with Jesus. I can't imagine worshiping a God who I couldn't talk to or hear from. Prayer is both of these things. It is talking to God and it is listening to God—as it is with all good communication. Worship is no different. It is both talking and listening. Again, it is revelation and response.

I love how Eugene Peterson describes the conversational nature of prayer when he says:

> Silence in prayer, which consists mostly of attentive listening, is nonnegotiable. Listening, which necessarily requires silence on our part, is as much a part of language as the words. The colon and the semicolon, the comma and the period— all of which insist on silence as part and parcel of speech—are as essential to language as nouns and verbs. But more often than not, silence gets short shrift in our prayers. Yet if there is no silence, our speech degenerates into babble.[11]

In the same way, to never wait on God in our worship lives, creates weak forms of worship and weak worshipers. As we pause, silence ourselves, and wait on God, we receive strength. The word 'wait' that the prophet Isaiah chose in Isaiah 40:31 means to hope for, to look for, and to look forward with confidence.[12] In those moments in our hiding away and seeking God's face (as well as in the corporate setting), where the music ebbs and the prayers or lyrics run out and we simply wait with confidence to see what God will do next... those are the moments where we exchange weariness for strength and a tired limp for an energised run. Musically, we need ebb and flow; crescendos and decrescendos. The musical rests play as big a role as the notes that are struck. Worship and prayer are exactly the same—both the noise and the silence matter.

In the previous chapter, we read John 10:27, which says, 'My sheep hear my voice, and I know them, and they follow me.' Let me state this again—hearing the voice of God is the right and inheritance of every child of God. It is *your* inheritance. If we don't first hear Him call, how can we, by definition, be following? We come to hear His voice and know His guidance in the intimate place of prayer and worship.

I remember at school when the office receptionist or the Principal would make an announcement over the loudspeaker that would go directly into every classroom and even carry to the surrounding streets of the suburb! We lived only a few streets away from my primary school in Brisbane, so even on my sick days, I could hear who was in trouble. Everybody knew that 'Johnny Smith from 3W' needed to report to the Principal's office when it was announced over the loudspeaker. But it's entirely something different, special and personal when we hide away and seek God's face and He speaks to us personally, one on one. Sure, we can hear God's voice in the corporate shoulder-to-shoulder setting, but the most precious whispers are the ones where there is no one else but you and Jesus... all alone. As we shut away, we develop that conversational friendship that is grown and developed in the secret place—when He speaks straight to our heart and gives us personal encouragement, direction and guidance.

In Matthew 6:6, we read, 'But when you pray, go into your room and shut the door and pray to your Father who is in secret. And your Father who sees in secret will reward you.' The room that Jesus was referring to was the only room in the house that had a lock on the door and no windows to the outside world. It was where everything of value to the family was stored and kept safe.[13] Why did Jesus tell His disciples to prioritise worshiping Him in this kind of setting? Because it was devoid of distractions.

In Bible times, people were distracted from worship by things like the preparation of food—like Martha was—or keeping up religious appearances or external motivations like the Pharisees. Today, in our post-modern world, our most common distractions are backlit and have ringtones! It's not to say that the Church isn't riddled with people like myself who are constantly fighting a Martha propensity to prefer a Mary worship life. Nor is it that I don't sometimes slip into the trap of measuring the strength of my prayer life by how many 'shandabas' and 'amens' I get from the front row. But for the most part, our biggest distractions today can be held in our hands and they ping alerts at us all day long. And so, Jesus encourages us to learn how to 'shut the door' on life's distractions so that we can encounter Him with clarity and focus.

Research conducted in 2016 by dscout showed that the average smartphone user touches their phone 2,617 times a day with 'heavy users' charting at 5,427 daily touches.[14] The average user engages in 76 separate phone sessions a day with use commencing at 7 am and consistently increasing until dinner time each day. Forty-three percent of this usage was on apps such as Facebook, Instagram and WhatsApp.

A 2017 study conducted by the McCombs School of Business concluded that 'the mere presence of one's smartphone reduces available cognitive capacity and impairs cognitive functioning'.[15] Throughout this study, one group of participants had their phones with them in the room while they took a test, while the other subject group had their phones in a different room. Those whose phones were in another room 'significantly outperformed those participants who had their phones in a pocket or bag'.[16]

Let's return now to the location that Jesus encouraged His followers to engage with when they worshiped Him—an inner room. A room devoid of distractions. A room where we shut the door on interruptions.

Be honest for a moment. How many phones do you think are present in your church each week? Mine is normally in my pocket! Sometimes it's even there when I preach or worship lead—I really want to delete that sentence, but I promised I would keep it real. Sometimes I even use my phone during my secret place devotional time to read my Bible or research facts about the Bible! Let's piece this all together. The mere presence of our smartphones in church or our inner room with Jesus reduces our ability to absorb the truths of Scripture and to encounter and love God with all our heart, soul, strength and mind—literally! When we approach our prayer time and our reading of God's Word, there is a posture that the Bible teaches us to take that is made virtually impossible by the presence of our phones and other distractions. Let's take a look.

The writer of Hebrews says this about the Word of God:

> For the word of God is living and active, sharper than any two-edged sword, piercing to the division of soul and of spirit, of joints and of marrow, and discerning the thoughts and intentions of the heart. And no creature is hidden from his sight, but all are naked and exposed to the eyes of him to whom we must give account. (Hebrews 4:12–13)

Importantly, the phrase 'naked and exposed' in the original Greek used in this passage, conveys an image that is important in how we approach the Word of God. When animals were sacrificed on an altar, the sacrificial animal was laid upside down and its neck pulled back with the throat exposed to the priest's knife. This is the imagery the original language depicts. It also paints a picture of a gladiator, who when defeated in gladiatorial battle was laid across the knee of the victor with his throat exposed ready for the deathblow.[17] The vulnerability of a sacrificial animal with its throat exposed to the priest, or a defeated gladiator laid across the knee of the victor, shows how we are to come with *our* most vulnerable parts—our hearts, laid bare ready for God to do surgery on us. This posture means we are to approach the reading of God's Word not for *information* but *formation*. To position ourselves behind a closed door, in the secret place, in a position of vulnerability where the surgeon can get our most vulnerable places and make us more like Him.

Our phones and other distractions stunt our spiritual formation. That is why worshiping with a hide and seek mindset and heart posture is so important for every believer. It literally makes us like Christ.

Let's talk for a moment about what that 'room' that Jesus speaks of to His disciples may look like for us today. It may have windows and it may not have a lockable door, but in today's context, it definitely should not be a place that we take our phones. If we just made this one decision—to leave our smartphones outside of our secret place with God—we would grow in our spiritual IQ exponentially. Sure, we might miss someone's post, but in reality, that post is most likely just someone else's show and tell.

Read back over that dscout research for a moment. Most of what we use our phones for is all about the show and tell moments of our lives. But worship is all about hiding away and seeking God's face. Don't get me wrong, I'm not suggesting you throw your phone away in some mass church religious burning ceremony, but I am advocating that we rid our worship lives of all distractions. This was of course the key to Mary's commendable worship life that testified of the 'one thing' that really matters (Luke 10:42).

Jesus modelled this kind of hide and seek worship life with His Father. In Luke 5:16 we read that Jesus 'would withdraw to desolate places and pray'. This word 'desolate' that Luke uses here is the word *eremos*. It speaks of an uninhabited, lonely, solitary, remote and deserted place with no inhabitants other than Him and His Father.[18] Jesus found himself a secret place, a place devoid of distractions, and we as His disciples must do the same thing. Sure, Jesus had a very public ministry that could have looked like a whole lot of show and tell to others, but it was all an overflow of His hide and seek worship life in the *eremos*. We, too, must have places and environments that are devoid of distraction and uninhabited, for ourselves and Jesus alone.

At the primary school that my children attended, like most other primary schools across Australia, there is a weekly award given out to one child from each class who has excelled in representing the school values for the past week. These values include things like being considerate, being a risk-taker, cooperating and being honest.

When my little hide and seek expert, Eden, was in pre-primary, she didn't manage to 'win' this award until term three. It was a long time to wait. In fact, she got so sick of waiting that there was a little bit of deceit involved! I remember the day she came bounding down the hill towards the car, backpack as big as her body, waving her little achievement ribbon in front of her. My first thought was, *Why didn't they send me an email telling me she was going to win?* This was the normal practice so that you could make sure you were at the school assembly as the award was presented, getting that all-important show and tell shot. I immediately thought I must have missed the email and made a mental note to check when I got home. Eden made a triumphant entrance to the car and told me all about what she had done to win the award and how it was 'about time'. We celebrated. We whooped and hollered. Our girl was the star student for the week. I quietly swallowed my feelings of failure that I had missed this important milestone in her life.

As I took a few moments after the dinner rush to check my email, I was puzzled to find that there was no email inviting me to attend the assembly—not even in my junk box. I decided to head up to school early the next morning and chat with the teacher and express my disappointment at missing this moment.

As I chatted with this beautiful educator, a little smirk began to appear on her face as I shared how I was so sad that I'd missed this moment in Eden's life. I could see that there was perhaps more to the story by the look on her face as she proceeded to tell me that the achievement ribbon for yesterday's assembly had gone missing off her desk partway through the day resulting in a mad rush to the school office to get a new one in time for the presentation to the real award winner...

who was not my daughter! I quickly apologised and shuffled away embarrassed. Not only had my daughter not won an award all year, but she was also a petty thief! My little trooper had gotten so sick of waiting to win and didn't quite get the concept of doing what was required to win a genuine award, so she just stole someone else's. I can laugh now, but at the time it wasn't very funny.

When it comes to the secret place, to our hide and seek lives of worship, we have to earn our own rewards. We just can't go stealing someone else's or taking short-cuts. The awesome news is that when we enter the secret place with the right heart motives, to simply spend time worshiping and communing with Jesus, 'your Father who sees in secret will reward you' (Matthew 6:6). It feels almost wrong to talk about being rewarded for spending time with God, doesn't it? Why is that? I think it's because we want to keep our motives pure and make sure we're not in it to get something other than just getting God, right? But here's the thing—Jesus had no issue talking about rewards. It's a biblical concept.

In Hebrews 11:6, we read that our Father 'rewards those who seek him'. He requires us to seek Him in the secret place to keep our motives pure, and then He rewards us very publicly. Pretty sweet deal, right? Now before you go thinking that you can 'secret place' yourself to the latest 'rarri, Jesus is, of course, talking about rewards of much higher value than any natural realm reward.

As I have grown in my personal worship and learned to *delight* in my daily disciplines in the secret place, the rewards in my life have been revelation, encounter and intimacy with Jesus that cannot be found any other way. Jesus said in Matthew 5:8, 'Blessed are the pure in heart, for they shall see God.' What greater reward is there than seeing God through the reading of His Word? What greater reward is there than hearing God's voice as we pray in the secret place? What could be better than being changed to be more like Jesus as we hide away and seek His face? There is no greater reward. And when we prize or value the public show and tell parts of our worship lives more than we do the hide and seek, we have become Pharisaical in our worship lives, and as we have learned, Jesus has much to say about this.

I have found that one of the biggest stumbling blocks to people's prayer lives as they develop a hide and seek life with God, is getting caught up on rating the effectiveness of their prayers. Are they praying long enough? Are they using enough theological words? Sure our prayer lives will mature and grow as we live life's journey, but we actually get better at praying, by praying! A one-word cry of 'Jesus' can be just as effective as a verbose, fifteen-minute prayer from the church's greatest prayer warrior. It's not about the words—it's all about the heart.

In Jesus' discourse on prayer, we read, 'And when you pray, do not heap up empty phrases as the Gentiles do, for they think that they will be heard for their many words' (Matthew 6:7). The particular context that Jesus was addressing here was the habit of the Gentiles in their prayers to pester their gods with repetitious babble where they would repeat the one phrase over and over, similar to the word 'abracadabra'.[19] This was necessary for the pagans because they did not know if they were praying to the right god, they were anxious about whether or not their god knew their needs, and they were trying to wear their god down by manipulating him through many words.[20]

But when we pray in the secret, hidden place, 'we have this confidence, we can also have great boldness before him, for if we present any request agreeable to his will, he will hear us' (1 John 5:14 TPT). Like all worship, prayer is all about the posture of the heart, not about the external measure of our eloquence of the word count. Now you can breathe a huge sigh of relief. It was never meant to be *sebo*.

One essential element of a personal hide and seek worship life that we don't talk about very often is walking in the covenant of forgiveness, and yet, this is a game-changer for walking in the freedom Christ has purchased for us.

One of my heroes, Neil T Anderson—who teaches brilliantly on freedom and identity in Christ—said this: 'In helping people find their freedom in Christ, I've come to see that unforgiveness is the number one basis for Satan having access to the Church.'[21] This is a very sobering thought given that included in Jesus' teaching on prayer is this statement: 'and forgive us our debts, as we also have forgiven our debtors' (Matthew 6:12). Here, Jesus links the forgiveness we receive and the forgiveness we give.

He goes on in verses 14–15 to say, 'For if you forgive others their trespasses, your heavenly Father will also forgive you, but if you do not forgive others their trespasses, neither will your Father forgive your trespasses.' Hold the phone everyone—if we do not offer forgiveness to others, we forfeit our right to receive forgiveness. Just think about that for a moment because that's a big statement. How often have you, like me, come into the secret place and prayed, worshiped God, read the Word, and not been walking in forgiveness? Probably more often than I care to admit.

When we don't walk in forgiveness towards others, and we then try to hide away and seek God's face, we actually take the person who we have not forgiven into our secret place with God. This is because unforgiveness ties us to the other person spiritually. In effect, we have made our hide and seek worship lives an exercise in show and tell because we've brought an audience with us into the secret place and their admission ticket was the unforgiveness residing in our hearts. This is why in Matthew 5:23–24, Jesus taught us, '…If you enter your place of worship and, about to make an offering, you suddenly remember a grudge a friend has against you, abandon your offering, leave immediately, go to this friend and make things right. Then and only then, come back and work things out with God' (MSG).

This is why it has become so important to me to approach my hide and seek worship life with regular times set aside to ask the Holy Spirit to examine my heart in the area of forgiveness. For me, this looks like an easy five-step process that you can incorporate into your Word, prayer and worship life. I set aside time on my Sabbath to go through these steps and I always feel much freer to worship on the other side.

The first step is to spend some time thanking God for your forgiveness. In Romans 3:23, we read that 'all have sinned and fall short of the glory of God'. This means that every one of us needed forgiveness from a Saviour to come into right relationship with God. And because of Jesus and His finished work on the cross, we now live free of condemnation and shame as forgiven children of God.

Spending some time in prayer thanking God for His forgiveness in your own life, helps you to be ready for the next step, which is to ask the Holy Spirit if there is anything hidden in your heart that you need to seek forgiveness for. I love to use King David's prayer from Psalm 139:23–24: 'Search me, O God, and know my heart! Try me and know my thoughts! And see if there be any grievous way in me, and lead me in the way everlasting!' Spend some time listening to the voice of the Holy Spirit and see what He brings up in you. Then, confidently ask your loving Father to forgive you for your sins, standing on this scriptural foundation: 'If we confess our sins, he is faithful and just to forgive us our sins and to cleanse us from all unrighteousness' (1 John 1:9).

Mindful now of your own encounter with the freedom of fresh forgiveness and a new beginning, we engage with step three, which is to ask God if there is anyone you are walking in unforgiveness towards. Again, allow the Holy Spirit to speak to you. Write down in a journal anyone or any specific situation He might bring to mind. It could be as simple as someone embarrassing you with a thoughtless comment in front of your peers, or as deep as a childhood wound. Whatever the Holy Spirit brings up, trust Him as your counsellor and write it down.

Then, spend some time journaling a prayer that extends forgiveness towards this person and read it out loud. I encourage you to name the person and the offence before God in a simple way such as, 'Lord, I forgive Jane for embarrassing me in that meeting this week when she said that I wouldn't understand what she was talking about. I want to be free from this offence.'

Another important aspect that I have found helpful in this step is to pray something along these lines: 'I release Jane from the expectation of ever giving me an apology because this is between me and you.' (P.S. No Janes were harmed in the writing of this book.) There may be times where the Holy Spirit asks you to do something that involves that other person, but more often than not, this can be between you and God alone.

The fifth and final step is to offer thanksgiving to God for walking you through this process so that you can now spend time in the secret place, hiding away and seeking His face alone—with no silent observers.

Regular examination practices around this area of forgiveness will change your worship life. Jesus felt that it was important enough to include in His teaching about prayer with His disciples and to include it in the passage where He addressed hypocrisy. After all, when we attempt to encounter Jesus and the freedom of His forgiveness in the secret place while not extending forgiveness to others, it is the ultimate act of hypocrisy.

I understand that forgiving people for deep wounds is not easy—believe me, I'm still working through my own stuff in this area—but forgiving someone doesn't make what they did okay. It just means that you don't want your prayer, Word and worship life to be show and tell when it's meant to be hide and seek.

Worship is hide and seek—never show and tell. Are you hiding away to seek His face?

— 9 —

WORSHIP IS
A Mirror

Worship is no longer worship when it reflects the culture around us more than the Christ within us.

A.W. TOZER [1]

Do you ever have those seasons in life when you can sense a distance between you and God? I don't mean those spiritually dry seasons, although there have been plenty of those too. I'm talking specifically about the times when you know there are some walls up between you and God that are causing you to avoid His presence. If you're anything like me, you'll also be intensely aware of who put the walls there—and we all know it isn't God. His business is removing walls. In fact, He specialises in it. In a nutshell, we're the only ones constructing walls, and usually, the individual bricks that make up these walls are labelled disappointment, offence, impatience, selfishness and the list goes on. Yep. Those seasons.

Sometimes, I'm even naive enough to believe that I know better than God, and when His plan differs from mine, I lay a brick in the wall. Sometimes people I love disappoint me or let me down, and somehow I hold God responsible, and in goes another brick. Before I know it, there's distance.

It is most often in the place of worship and surrender that those walls in my life have come tumbling down, and I have found myself able to see God clearly and receive His perspective on what I am facing. I remember a moment following my second miscarriage, when I was quietly crying on the couch, and the Holy Spirit said, 'Go to the piano and worship me.' I'd love to say that I obeyed straight away, but to be honest, worship was too painful and vulnerable and I didn't feel ready to give the pain full permission to come to the surface.

Eventually, after arguing with God, I sat down at the piano and wrote a song called 'You Cover Me'. I didn't even believe at the time the lyrics that flowed out of me, but God was gifting me with a faith song to sing over myself until I could declare it as truth for myself, and eventually for others. Within twelve months, I got to sing that song as part of our church's television program where we covered the story of a beautiful couple in ministry who tragically lost their little boy before he was even one year old. I got to sing these lyrics over them:

> You are the peace that quiets me.
> You are the strength that lights my way.
> You light my way.
>
> I look to You. I'll never thirst.
> I'll trust in You, You cover me.
> You cover me.

Jesus, Jesus.
I yearn for You. You're all I need.
Jesus, Jesus. I long for You.
You're all I need.
You're all I need.

You lead me by still waters.
Restore my soul.
You lead me by still waters.
Restore my soul.
You're all I need.[2]

It was simple, but it was all I could manage in that season. Yes, I sang those words before I believed them, but as I positioned myself in worship, and God revealed His great love to me, my desire to ask 'why' decreased. As He revealed His love in all its depth, width and height, I didn't need to understand because I just knew that I was loved, and that was enough. It took time, but the walls came down, and on the other side of my test, I had a testimony to sing.

The problem with allowing those walls to remain is that while they are there, we cannot fully receive from God all that He wants to pour into our lives, let alone reflect Christ to others around us. It is only when all those walls come tumbling down, brick by brick, that we can become more Christlike, therefore becoming a true reflection of Christ to those around us. And worship is the pathway to both outcomes. Another way to put it is this: those walls that we allow to be constructed in our hearts will stop us from maturing in Christ and from being an effective witness for Christ. Again, the answer to both dilemmas is worship.

In the book of Joshua, we see biblical precedent for worship being the key to breakthrough in eradicating walls of containment in our lives. The Israelites have finally crossed over into the Promised Land and are primed to conquer Jericho when God issues a rather strange set of instructions for conquest. Joshua, an accomplished military leader was now not to rely on his experience in warfare, but to display unwavering obedience to the specific commandments God gave him. Joshua was commanded not to use ordinary weapons of warfare such as battering rams or ladders, but instead to march around the city for six successive days in silence, other than the noise of marching feet and seven priests blowing 'jubilee trumpets'.

These trumpets were typically used to proclaim the presence of God at Israel's solemn feasts. In this instance, they were used to signify to every person hiding within the walls of this great city that God's presence was encircling them, and their defeat was imminent. The trumpets were not the only symbol of God's sovereign presence that paraded repeatedly around the city—the ark of the covenant followed it closely behind.[3] Just as in other settings, the ark symbolised God's presence with His people.[4]

Can you imagine being walled up in the city and for six days hearing nothing but marching feet and the sound of warfare trumpets? It's a pretty intimidating scenario. On the seventh day, the Israelites were commanded to march around the city seven times:

> 'Shout, for the LORD has given you the city.'

> …So the people shouted, and the trumpets were blown. As soon as the people heard the sound of the trumpet, the people shouted a great shout, and the wall fell down flat, so that the people went up into the city, every man straight before him, and they captured the city. (Joshua 6:16, 20)

Archaeological excavation of this particular site has revealed that it was not only the walls of Jericho that fell flat that day but that walls in several locations fell flat at the sound of the trumpet blast and the seemingly nonsensical faith shout of the people of God.[5] This is a beautiful scene of worship in the midst of adversity, despite natural and human logic. This is because the conquest of Jericho was not just a military undertaking, but both personal and corporate worship warfare.[6] As the trumpets blasted and the shout was released against the walls of this great city, the spiritual realm was filled with echoes of Psalm 24:7 when David penned lyrics to accompany the ark being brought into Jerusalem: 'Lift up your heads, O gates! And be lifted up, O ancient doors, that the King of glory may come in.'

When we sense walls in our hearts, but we choose to worship, we are ruling our souls and spirits, commanding our hearts to 'let the King of glory come in'. It is then, with freed up hearts that are no longer segmented by walls of disappointment or shame and condemnation, that we can begin to reflect this glory to the world around us, as we were created to.

Paul teaches that when the secrets of our hearts are disclosed, our response will be to worship.[7] Sometimes we're not even aware of why we have constructed walls of defence in our hearts, so it's a good practice when you sense that distance to ask the Holy Spirit to show you what may be hidden inside of you and to allow your response to be worship. This can be as simple as praying, 'Create in me a clean heart… and renew a right spirit within me'.[8] To receive discernment of the source of the wall is a good thing, but the goal is to *remove* the wall so that we can both *receive* and *reflect* God's glory. Like it was for the Israelites, the strategy and the weapon is worship.

Author and worship Granddaddy, Ray Hughes, powerfully describes the war for worship that originated in the heart of the first worship leader, Lucifer. As we've already discovered, Lucifer was an angel whose name meant 'light bearer'. Many commentators believe that Lucifer did not need to pick up a musical instrument to lead worship because his very being had the ability to make the sounds of all the instruments required to bring worship to God. These Christian scholars state that all the sounds of Heaven and earth resided in his very being.

Lucifer also wore a breastplate that contained stones that were designed to reflect the glory of God.[9]

Lucifer, stationed as one of three archangels within the throne room of God, was to direct his body towards the throne, capture God's glory and then reflect it to all of God's creation and humanity so that they could then respond to God's glory in turn. This was his role as the worship leader and it still is the role of a worship leader and every single worshiper today—that's you and me.

The problem was, pride entered Lucifer's heart and he wanted to keep the glory for himself. One who was created to be a reflection of God's glory instead chose to absorb it into his own heart and being, and it eventually destroyed his calling. If we make the same choices when it comes to our worship, it will ultimately destroy our calling too.

Hughes, in speaking of the moment when Satan was cast out of Heaven, says, 'If pride turned angels into demons, guess what it will do to you and me.'[10] We were never intended to absorb God's glory and not pass it on. We are all designed and created to reflect God in all His glory to the world around us. We are, in a sense, mirror images of God. But to be accurate reflections, we must first encounter His glory. As we have already discovered, we *become* what we *behold*. In simple terms, we cannot give away what we have not already received. God can only do *through* us what He has already done *in* us.

Let me remind you that in Genesis 1:27 we read, 'So God created man in his own image, in the image of God he created him; male and female he created them.' This word 'image' is the word *selem*. It means to be made in God's likeness, patterned and modelled after our Father God.[11]

In the New Testament, the Greek word used for 'image' is the word *eikon*. Similarly, this word describes having the same form as something else. Looking at how this word was used in the Greco Roman culture, which we get a peek into throughout the Gospels, we can see God's intent for us, His children, who are created in His *eikon*.[12] A denarius was a coin used within the Roman Empire that was stamped with the *eikon* of Caeser. This inscription of the Roman leader on the denarii *identified* the *authenticity* and *value* of the coins. The imagery here is that you and I are stamped as exact replicas of our Heavenly Father, and therefore, this is what gives us our sense of identity and value.

In Colossians 1:15, we read that Jesus is 'the image of the invisible God'. There we have that word again. Jesus is the *eikon* of His Father. The writer of Hebrews describes Jesus this way: 'He is the radiance of the glory of God and the exact imprint of his nature' (Hebrews 1:3). Take a moment and let that sink in. Jesus is the exact imprint of God in nature and character. We, in our purest, original Eden-like state, were also created this way. Selah. Pause. Take a breath and meditate on that.

When we understand that we are an exact imprint of God, just like Jesus, and that we are a coin stamped with the image and imprint of our King who determines our identity and our value, it will change the way we live and approach life. By design, we are created to reflect and mirror God to the world around us, just like Jesus did.

The problem is this: you and I, just like the 'unrighteous' people that Paul referred to in his letter to the

Romans, have 'exchanged the glory of the immortal God for images [eikons] resembling mortal man...' (Romans 1:23). In this passage, Paul was referring to pagan idol worship, but we can apply this to our lives today. We have been given an eternal identity because we are created in the image of an immortal, invisible, eternal God. And yet, we so often exchange or lay down this eternal image for an external, imposed image that is temporary and fleeting.

When we allow the world's culture, other people's opinions, and the values of our society rather than Kingdom culture to determine our value, we become a foolish person who hears the Word and truth of God about our identity but does not apply it. In Matthew 7:27, we read of the foolish man who did just that—heard the Word but did not apply it: 'The rain fell, and the floods came, and the winds blew and beat against that house, and it fell, and great was the fall of it.' The thing is, we want our walls to fall down, not the whole house! This does not mirror God well to our world. James says it like this:

> For if anyone is a hearer of the word and not a doer, he is like a man who looks intently at his natural face in a mirror. For he looks at himself and goes away and at once forgets what he was like. (James 1:23–24)

In Genesis 3, when Eve and Adam gave in to the accusation, questioning and deception of the serpent, their vision changed. How they saw the world was altered, how they saw God was corrupted, and how they saw themselves was compromised. Before their sin, they only saw the world as God saw it. But in believing the deception of the serpent, they sacrificed their heavenly perspective for the viewpoint of the serpent that slithered in the dirt on its belly. They lost perspective and got caught up in the mud of life.

In Genesis 3:6, we read, 'So when the woman saw that the tree was good for food, and that it was a delight to the eyes, and that the tree was to be desired to make one wise, she took of its fruit and ate, and she also gave some to her husband who was with her, and he ate.' Here it comes. Cue dramatic music—'Then the eyes of both were opened' (verse 7).

This is quite a contradictory little passage. We first read that the tree was a 'delight to the eyes', which indicates that both Adam and Eve had no issue with their natural vision. But after giving in to the deception and eating the fruit, 'the eyes of both were opened'. Let's drill down here for a moment.

In the original language, this does not indicate that their eyes were ever closed or that they suffered from any form of natural blindness, but spiritually they were unable to see anything other than good before sin.[13] Isn't this just one of the saddest little verses in the whole book that we love? Because ever since, we have struggled to regain the ability to see the world, others and ourselves from Heaven's perspective and to believe that we truly are the exact imprint of His nature, just as Jesus was. And just like Adam and Eve, we have struggled with shame and condemnation in our worship lives ever since. We know that Adam and Eve would walk in the garden with God in the cool of the day, but once their perception of self changed, they sewed clothing for themselves in an attempt to cover their sin and shame and 'hid themselves from the presence of the Lord God' (Genesis 3:8).

I have found that we tend to do the same thing. We start to believe the accusations of the enemy that are coming at us day and night,[14] and it changes our perception of ourselves and God's world. It changes our vision. And then we cover ourselves, and we hide in shame, we allow walls to be built, and we avoid God's presence. The thing is, while we're cloaked in shame and hiding behind a tree, we can't mirror God to the world around us. While we avoid the light and hideaway in the shadows, we can't reflect the One who is light.

Here's the good news... Jesus came and He changed *everything*! Not only did our Great High Priest's saving work on the cross make a way for you and me to come boldly without shame,[15] but He then gave us the Holy Spirit to help us to once again awaken to our true identity as exact replicas of our Father God. In fact, we will spend the rest of our lives being transformed into the fullness of this image. We will spend the rest of our lives restoring Eden.

In 2 Corinthians 3:18, we read, 'And we all, with unveiled face, beholding the glory of the Lord, are being transformed into the same image from one degree of glory to another. For this comes from the Lord who is the Spirit.' We've already covered the fullness of this Scripture, but in this context, let's take a little refresher.

This word 'behold' means to reflect—to reflect God's glory; to mirror His glory to the world. We do this with increasing effectiveness as we go through the process of being transformed, like a caterpillar to a butterfly, and this is all facilitated by the work of the Holy Spirit when we position ourselves in worship. Eugene Peterson phrases it this way: '…our lives gradually becoming brighter and more beautiful as God enters our lives and we become like him' (2 Corinthians 3:18 MSG). So, we see that worship mirrors the true state of our lives back to us, it reveals walls and obstacles and it transforms us back into our Eden-like state where we can reflect or mirror God to the world around us. In living this way, we embody Paul's appeal in Romans 12:1–2:

> I appeal to you therefore, brothers, by the mercies of God, to present your bodies as a living sacrifice, holy and acceptable to God, which is your spiritual worship. Do not be conformed to this world, but be transformed by the renewal of your mind, that by testing you may discern what is the will of God, what is good and acceptable and perfect.

When we daily choose to keep showing up in the place of intimate worship before God, and offer our lives to Him, it is the ultimate act of love and adoration. The word used for worship here is the word *latreia*, which means to minister to God.[16] When we come back to the place of worship, without walls, without hiding, but living in the fullness of what Jesus did for us, it ministers to the heart of God. We become the Priests and Levites before God.[17] As we make the choice to not conform to the culture of this world, but to mirror God effectively through transformational worship, we become the royal priesthood described in 1 Peter 2:9 who 'proclaim the excellencies of him who called you out of darkness into his marvelous light'.

Our effectiveness to mirror Him well comes as our minds are renewed in the hide and seek place of worship. As we discussed in Chapter 6, this word 'transformed' is the same word from 2 Corinthians 3:18 which describes the metamorphosis process. Think about the visual perspective of a caterpillar. Similar to the serpent, it doesn't have a high vantage point from which to observe life. However, the butterfly, in all her beauty, enjoys big picture vision similar to the viewpoint of Heaven.

We are designed to live here as Adam and Eve did before the corruption of their worship lives. And through the help of the Holy Spirit, we are invited back to this place of perspective and freedom in our worship. Worship may indeed reveal to us that we have accepted the lie that we must see the world from the position of a caterpillar or serpent, lying in the dust and mess of life, but the Holy Spirit invites us to be restored to our original position and identity where we have God's thoughts and vision about ourselves and the world. We find this mountain top view in His presence.

When my baby girl was around two years old, we went Christmas shopping. We needed to head up a few floors in a large department store, and the escalators were broken. We stood at the elevator doors with what felt like half of Melbourne. When the lift doors finally opened, I took her by the hand and headed into the crowded lift. In all honestly, there probably wasn't enough room for us, but I wasn't waiting any longer. So I stood, pressed face to face with the crowd, and Eden stood with her face pressed against a bunch of kneecaps and thighs. We didn't even have room to turn around and put our backs to people. I looked down at Eden as she began to cry. I bent down to pick her up, and immediately, the tears dried and her little face lit up in a big smile and she said, 'We go shopping now Mummy.' What had changed? We were in the same lift with the same crowded mess of humanity, but she had a new vantage point—the safety of her mummy's hip.

This is a picture of what happens to us when we worship. We may be acutely aware of the dirt and mess of our lives, the walls that we have allowed to be constructed, and our sin and shame. But as we begin to lift our praise and our worship to the One who has stamped us with His very nature, we come higher and realign with our eternal identity, and we shine so the whole world can see His glory.

I'm going to speak honestly for a moment to the Church because I'm sure you know my heart for the Bride by now and can hear that these words are motivated by love. I so often have people approach me before and after services or via email telling me what they don't like about the song selection, the lights, the cameras, the singers, the worship leaders, the drums and many other things. I hear people's hearts and I know we grow through feedback, but here's the thing: our worship was never meant to mirror our likes, preferences or dislikes. Worship was never intended to be a service *for* us. Worship is meant to mirror God's likes, God's truth, God's nature and God's glory. Worship is our service and our ministry to Him. God is not called to reflect us; we are called to reflect Him. We are made in His image and called to bring Heaven to earth by walking in the fullness of our eternal identity.

Worship is a mirror. It's a mirror held up to our hearts so that we can be free from shame, condemnation and separation. Worship is a life that chooses to gaze at Jesus and catch a glimpse of His reflection and then bounce back praise and adoration at what He reveals. As we do this, as He reveals Himself and we respond, we become more like Him and then we mirror Him to a world that needs Him desperately.

Let's bring this home by personalising our opening Tozer quote: does your worship reflect the culture around you or Christ within you? Worship is a mirror. Who is your worship reflecting?

WORSHIP IS
Both/And

Worship is not part of the Christian life,
it is the Christian life.

GERALD VANN [1]

One of my favourite moments is when I meet new people and they ask that inevitable question: 'So what do you do for work?' It doesn't take long for us to move to this topic, does it? It normally comes up straight after you learn each other's names. I don't have the luxury of making small talk with people because what I do for work naturally lends to getting straight to the heart of the matter. We jump straight to the 'make or break' moment right after I clarify that it's 'Stacey' and not 'Tracey'. That's why I've learned to just be straight up with my answer and know once and for all if this person is ever going to speak to me again. My answer usually goes something like this: 'I'm a pastor at a church and I work with all of the creatives and prophetic people.' Cue crickets, awkward smiles and slowly backing away.

For people who understand church life though, it's easy for them to imagine my everyday life of prayer, continuous Bible reading and memorisation, fasting and abstinence, silence, contemplation and worship all the sweet day long with a symphony of angelic hosts bathed in golden light when I let them know that I'm 'in ministry'. Or perhaps you're more like my kids who think I do nothing but have coffees with people all week long and occasionally write a song or a sermon. One thing is for sure, it's much easier to imagine someone who is in 'full-time ministry' living all of their life in surrendered worship than it is to imagine the dad in IT or the young professional who just made junior partner at a law firm. Perhaps this is because the prevailing belief within our culture today is that there is, and should be, a divide between the secular and the sacred.

Interestingly, you will find no such division within the pages of your Bible. Historically, modernism or the enlightenment of the 17th–19th centuries, saw a transition from living according to faith-based beliefs and biblical truth to an elevation of human reasoning, empiricism and logic. Modernism soon replaced Christianity as the dominant worldview as philosophers such as Immanuel Kant presented radical views that divided reality into two parts: the *phenomenal*, which is the world of fact and human reasoning, and the *noumenal* representing morality and spirituality. He believed that within this spiritual realm, no factual or logical basis provided certainty, and therefore these things should be kept private and outside of the public domain.[2]

Essentially, God was eliminated from the public arena and 'human reasoning replaced God in determining moral laws'.[3] Eventually, this led to an accepted societal norm that our jobs or our roles in the marketplace are completely separate from our lives of worship. Even if we take the average number of hours that full-time working Australians worked per week in 2019—that is thirty-nine hours a week[4] devoid of God if we submit to our prevailing world culture of secular, sacred separation. However, according to what Scripture teaches, we cannot divorce the sacred and the secular, and we were never intended to.[5] Author John Mark Comer describes the transition this way:

> The sacred/secular divide is this erroneous idea that some things are sacred or spiritual, and they matter to God; but other things are secular or physical, and by implication, they don't matter to God... The problem with this widespread, ubiquitous, domineering, destructive way of thinking is that, well, by this definition, most of life is secular... In the church, we often spend the majority of our time teaching people how to live the minority of their lives.[6]

Recent studies showed that the biggest deterrent to Australians engaging with Christianity 'is the Church's stance and teaching on homosexuality', with 31 percent of respondents saying that this blocked their interest in the Church and God.[7] Although there are many considerations involved with this particular issue, including the Church's sometimes mishandling of this issue or inability to communicate love, this research really does point to the prevailing cultural idea that the sacred should have no influence or voice in how we live life or on the secular. However, in God's Kingdom, all of our lives, our work lives, our family lives, our sporting club involvement, even our house cleaning, can be worship before God.

The Apostle Paul wrote to one of the most secular societies of the day:[8] 'I appeal to you therefore, brothers, by the mercies of God, to present your bodies as a living sacrifice, holy and acceptable to God, which is your spiritual worship' (Romans 12:1). This isn't the first time we've visited this verse in our time together, which is not surprising because this particular Scripture is one of the most formative in how we should live our lives as worshipers and as followers of Christ. Paul is speaking about the relationship between Christian belief and practice. In other words, he is speaking to us of a life with no secular sacred divide, rather a life that is congruent all the way through, and he describes a life lived this way as 'spiritual worship'.[9]

In speaking of our 'bodies' as *living* sacrifices, Paul is addressing our whole life and activities, not just our physical bodies. The problem is, you and I keep on getting off the altar (that's generally the problem with a living sacrifice). Our lives are worship to God when we continually lay down our will and our little kingdoms for His will and His Kingdom. This kind of life offered in worship is holy and pleasing to God. It is 'sacred service'.[10] It is clear that to Paul, and us as Christians today, that all of our life can be an act of worship and service to God:

So, whether you eat or drink, or whatever you do,
do all to the glory of God. (1 Corinthians 10:31)

Whatever you do, in word or deed, do everything
in the name of the Lord Jesus, giving thanks to
God the Father through him. (Colossians 3:17)

From the very beginning, God intended even our work lives to be worship. In Genesis 2:15, that immediately follows the creation of man, 'The LORD God took the man and put him in the garden of Eden to work it and keep it.' This word 'work' is the word *abad*. Its literal meaning is to worship or to serve.[11] Let's catch the significance of this.

Prior to sin entering the world, when everything was literally 'all g', Adam was placed in paradise and given the task of working, and his work was his worship. Adam didn't have a compartmentalised life that was either work or worship; his work was his worship. It wasn't either/or. It was both/and. He was also given the task of 'keeping' the garden, which is the word *samar* meaning to guard, care for and secure something.[12] In other words, Adam's worship was guarding, caring for, taking care of 'property in trust'[13] and securing the territory God had assigned to him. This was the original design for the work of man's hand and when we approach our work this way today, we restore Eden. We bring Kingdom to earth.

I hope by now, you are seeing the big idea woven throughout these pages—worship is the *vehicle* that will bring Kingdom to earth. We are the *vessels*, submitted and yielded as an act of worship that will outwork God's big dream. Author Daniel Block puts it this way: 'To be human is to work, and to work is worship. Work is the principal act of worship to which human beings are called.'[14]

Pause here for a moment and reflect on what territory or 'property in trust' you have been given to steward as an act of worship. Do you have children? They are yours to steward as worship. Are you married? This relationship is yours to cultivate as an act of worship. Do you work in an architectural firm? This is your garden to guard, care for and secure as an act of worship to God. It is not a place where you hide your love for God or the fact that you go to church. Instead, as a holistic spiritual being, you worship by how you approach what you have been entrusted with, and you 'take your everyday, ordinary life—your sleeping, eating, going-to-work, and walking-around life—and place it before God as an offering' (Romans 12:1 MSG).

Jesus taught us in Matthew 22:37 to 'Love the Lord your God with every passion of your heart, with all the energy of your being, and with every thought that is within you' (TPT). This is not the language of a compartmentalised life. God never intended to only be a small part of your life. He wants to bring health, wisdom, revelation and light to every part of who you are. He can only do this when we give Him access to every part of us.

Answering your emails can be just as much an act of 'Kingdom come' as when you are standing in church singing your favourite worship song. I hope by now, you can see that worship is so much more than the songs we sing. It's a life laid down, out of love and adoration to a God who has changed everything for you and me.

God's Kingdom is not a segmented, partially effective kingdom. He either reigns fully in our lives, or He doesn't reign at all. We either worship Him in how we do our finances, our relationships, our work and our building of His Church, or we don't worship Him at all. He wants it all. We don't live in a time or world where this is an easy way to live. It is very counter-cultural. While our Church history is drenched in lives that were 'all in' or 'all out', we live in a society that would prefer it if we kept our faith to ourselves, thank you very much. This is why praying and singing prayers as King David did in Psalm 86:11–13 are so important:

> Train me, God, to walk straight;
> then I'll follow your true path.
> Put me together, one heart and mind;
> then, undivided, I'll worship in joyful fear.
> From the bottom of my heart I thank you, dear
> Lord; I've never kept secret what you're up to.
> You've always been great toward me—what love!
> (MSG)

Nothing is more detrimental to God's reputation than hypocritical Christianity—a life that is not congruent or a mouth that professes one message and yet acts out of another ruling spirit that presides within the heart. That is why we need to continue to commit to developing our secret place, hide and seek worship lives that the rest of life flows from if we are to represent God well outside the four walls of the church. We can no longer hide in the safety of our church buildings or homes, professing our love for God and it not affect how we approach our shopping in the supermarket, loving our neighbour or how we approach our work lives. This would be to submit to the culture of the world that tells us that there is no place for the sacred in the secular. God's mandate for us as worshipers is that the sacred Kingdom of God rules the secular, not the other way around. The scales are tipped as we each make this choice in our personal lives.

As you and I choose to carry Kingdom, and as more people come to know Jesus through the overflow of our worship lives in our workplaces, schools, universities and sporting clubs, and then they start to carry Kingdom, soon the earth begins to once again look like Eden and reflect the atmosphere of Heaven. Darlene Zschech says it this way: 'When we worship Jesus, we declare His Kingdom and announce His presence.'[15] When you live a lifestyle of worship, you declare His Kingdom and announce His presence wherever your feet tread.

Our work is our worship. Our parenthood is our worship. How we do friendship is worship. How you practice the law or teach those students as a teacher, that is your worship. Daniel Block says, 'True worship is expressed primarily in everyday conduct.'[16] I once heard someone say that if you are a full-time Christian, you are in full-time ministry. Most of our lives are lived outside the four walls of the church. If we divide and compartmentalise our worship of God to what we do at church alone, we would prevent Him from being involved in most of our lives. We must understand that biblically, it's not either/or. It's both/and. It's the whole of our lives. It's every part of us postured in worship to our King. This is Kingdom come to earth. Worship is both/and.

The book of Ezekiel records a series of prophetic messages from a man who was both a priest and a prophet. Ezekiel was a prophet to those who were in exile in Babylon at one of the most critical times in the history of Israel. He was an exile prophesying to other exiles.[17]

During this time of upheaval and trauma, Jerusalem and her temple were captured and destroyed. Towards the end of his book of prophecies, Ezekiel is led by an angelic being on a visionary tour of the new, restored temple, which would be rebuilt once God had gathered His exiles back together to vindicate them.

In a Scripture we have already discussed, Ezekiel is brought to the entrance of the temple and shown a stream of water flowing out from underneath the threshold. As he walks by the water with his guide, he notices that the stream quickly becomes a river of significant depth. He also observes that the water flowing from the temple gives life and renewal everywhere it flows.[18] This prophetic vision is significant given that there were no natural springs or sources of water, but this stream was clearly supernatural in origin, and importantly, grew deeper the further it flowed from the temple. One commentator summarises the vision this way: 'This is surely a picture of the power of God's presence in his temple and among his people. It affects everything for good.'[19]

In John 7:38–39, I believe Jesus had this picture in mind:

'Whoever believes in me, as the Scripture has said, "Out of his heart will flow rivers of living water." Now this he said about the Spirit…'

Did you catch that? We house the Holy Spirit, and therefore, we are living, breathing, walking sources of living water. The further outside of the church we venture, the more the living water is needed. God's provision for us is that the depth will grow as we, 'Go therefore and make disciples of all nations, baptizing them in the name of the Father and of the Son and of the Holy Spirit, teaching them to observe all that I have commanded you' (Matthew 28:19–20).

In the same way that the celestial guide called Ezekiel's attention to the rapidly increasing stream by asking him, 'Son of man, have you seen this?' (Ezekiel 47:6), I believe the Spirit of God would ask you and I the same thing today. Do we have eyes to see what God is doing at this time? It is not enough for us to come to church shoulder to shoulder or to our private place of hide and seek where we meet with God face to face and just drink the living water. This is the best foundation, of course, but God has set us on a mission. He has given us a job to do here on earth, and we risk becoming like

'Tiddalick the Frog' if we hold all of that living water inside while people are dying of thirst around us. Hang on—did I lose you there? Let me explain.

Tiddalick the Frog is an Aboriginal Dreamtime story that is passed down through Indigenous generations to ensure Aboriginal spiritual beliefs about existence are transferred from one generation to another.[20] Sound familiar? It sounds like our Patriarchs in Deuteronomy 11:18 that were commanded to know God's words of instruction and to pass them on to future generations. Well, this story is a similar practice for the Australian Aborigines.

Back to the largest frog in the world—Tiddalick. One morning he woke up very thirsty and hopped his way to the local billabong where he drank the entire water supply. Soon, as the other Aussie animals started to wake and head for their morning sip, they found the water all dried up. Immediately knowing who had taken all of the water, the echidna, kookaburra, kangaroo and emu came up with the genius plan of trying to make Tiddalick laugh, to get him to let all of the water out! But nothing worked until finally, the snake came and tied himself up in knots, which the larger than life frog found amusing. Soon the water came gushing forth for others to drink as Tiddalick's chuckle turned into a full belly laugh as the snake continued to tie itself in knots as a comedy act.[21]

A random little story I know, but as I prayed in the quiet of our dark church one day and asked God what He was doing and saying to His Church, this is the story that He reminded me of. I have to admit, I hadn't thought about that story since grade three, and I questioned God. What on earth could He possibly be saying? Then He reminded me of Ezekiel's vision and Jesus' encounter with the woman at the well and it all began to make sense. Our world desperately needs the living water we have inside of us that Jesus spoke of with the woman at the well:

> '...whoever drinks of the water that I will give him will never be thirsty again. The water that I give him will become in him a spring of water welling up to eternal life.' The woman said to him, 'Sir, give me this water, so that I will not be thirsty or have to come here to draw water.' (John 4:13–15)

As true worshipers of our God, we have a spring of water inside of us that isn't just for private consumption. It's meant to be a spring for others. A spring that may start as a nervous trickle, but as we learn to open our mouth wide and let out our testimony of what God has done in our lives, it soon becomes a torrent—a river that brings life and healing to everybody we encounter. And the further out of the church we venture, the deeper and more effective it becomes.

There have been so many times when I have personally become a 'fat frog' just concerning myself with me, myself and I, and what I'm getting from God in my worship life. Sure, there are seasons when we need to get back to the basics of our intimacy with God, but Jesus has commissioned us in Matthew 5:13 as 'the salt of earth'. Notice He doesn't say we are the salt of the church. In fact, there is nothing worse than when you go to season your poached eggs with salt, and too much comes out in one spot.

Salt is only good for flavour when it is evenly distributed across the plate, and yet, we the Church love to pile ourselves up in one little corner, within the safety of our own little communities. But when we get outside the four walls into our workplaces, into our communities, into the land that God has given us to steward and *abad* and *selem*, our saltiness makes people thirsty. And thirsty people will soon look to find a water source. And guess what? A person that has saturated and immersed themself in a lifestyle of worship is a spring of life to everyone around them. A spring of life at the board table. A spring of life at the school kiss and drop. A spring of life in the grandstand. It's not either/or. It's both/and.

In Revelation 22:1–5, John had a visionary encounter about a source of water. He, just like Zeke, was shown by an angel, a river that flowed from the throne of God in the New Jerusalem. John described it this way:

> Then the angel showed me the river of the water of life, bright as crystal, flowing from the throne of God and of the Lamb through the middle of the street of the city; also, on either side of the river, the tree of life with its twelve kinds of fruit, yielding its fruit each month. The leaves

of the tree were for the healing of the nations. No longer will there be anything accursed, but the throne of God and of the Lamb will be in it, and his servants will worship him. They will see his face, and his name will be on their foreheads. And night will be no more. They will need no light of lamp or sun, for the Lord God will be their light, and they will reign forever and ever.

I have to admit that I find it near impossible to read this vision without getting emotional because it is the culmination moment where Eden will be restored, and my heart longs for that. Once again, the river of life will flow, there will be healing for the nations and we will all worship face to face.

In Matthew 3:11, John the Baptist said, 'I baptize you with water for repentance, but he who is coming after me is mightier than I, whose sandals I am not worthy to carry. He will baptize you with the Holy Spirit and fire.' This passage describes us being immersed, plunged, saturated and dripping with the Holy Spirit.[22] This immersion has a purpose—to equip us to leave the safety of our Christian and personal worship communities and get outside the temple, carrying the river of life out of our personal little Eden's so that more of the earth will be restored to its original design. This is us living in action and deed: 'Our Father in heaven, hallowed be your name. Your kingdom come, your will be done, on earth as it is in heaven' (Matthew 6:9–10).

Throughout the pages of this book, I pray that you have picked up that this has been the vision, the picture and the purpose that has kept me, held me and helped me to stand firm when I have wanted to fall or run away. One day, Eden will be restored in all its fullness and what a glorious day it will be. Meanwhile, I will spend my life preparing for eternity by bringing as much of it here as I can. I will do this by continuing to give my life to Him in worship—every part of my life—all of it.

Here is something you and I must consider: will this river that Ezekiel and John have seen, in a moment of worship, flow out from the temple or from God's throne in and of itself, or is God inviting you and I to literally walk it out into the marketplace, the community and the world?

I'm sure God could do this supernaturally, but as both a student of history and the Word of God, I see more evidence that God wants to use us to fulfill His dream that 'the earth will be filled with the knowledge of the glory of the LORD as the waters cover the sea' (Habakkuk 2:14).

You see, worship isn't only about our own personal healing, breakthrough, individual freedom, or our isolated church communities, moments of stillness, face-to-face encounters or even our hide and seek. Worship is a place to be equipped and filled to overflow with the living water so that we *fill the earth with the knowledge of the glory of God.* We don't just fill the church—we fill the earth. It's not either/or. It's both/and.

STUDY QUESTIONS

As you approach this section of the book where we dive a little deeper into some of the content and seek to apply it, I suggest you first journal your responses privately before taking it to a group or discipleship context. This will help you get more out of it and allow you time to process with the Holy Spirit. As with anything, you will get as much out of these reflection prompts as you put in. Enjoy!

Introduction: 'Caption This', Worship Is Biblical

1. Caption this—'Worship is...' Take some time to journal what worship is to you personally, what worship is to your creative team, and what worship is to your church family. Share your captions with one another.

2. Looking at the biblical definitions of *halal* and *tehila*, talk about whether or not you incorporate this personally in your worship life. How do you think your church family responds to being led in these specific applications of worship? Discuss if there is any room for growth in your life or in the life of your church for these expressions. What are some practical ways you could personally and corporately grow in this space?

3.   As a musician, singer or creative, do you ever practice *zamar*? Do you ever lay aside your words and just make a melody to God in response to His attributes and saving work in your life? Talk about any moments in your personal or corporate worship where you have experienced being led this way. Discuss how the instruments and voices reflected God's character. Think about whether or not there are ways you can grow artistically to reflect more attributes of God's nature. E.g. how would you sing love? How would you play the presence of the Prince of Peace? What instruments would feature if God came like a rushing wind? What does it sound like when God comes to heal?

4.   Looking at the definition of *threskeia*, reflect on your individual practice of worshiping by caring for orphans and widows. Is there room for you to grow in this? What about your creative team? Do you do anything proactive to worship God by serving orphans and widows? Does your church community do anything in this space, and is your creative team involved? Brainstorm some ways you could further practice this expression of worship.

5.   Of all the definitions provided from both the Old and New Testament, which one resonates with you the most? Why? Chat about this together and as you go about your next few days, ask the Holy Spirit to help you grow in your ability to worship God in diverse and biblical ways.

Chapter One: Worship Is Medicine

1. Has music ever been your medicine? Have you ever been healed in worship? Do you know of someone who has been healed in worship? What about music therapy? What do you know about that? Share your testimonies.

2. Read and discuss the evidence-based studies from Chapter 1 that describe the benefits for our well-being, health and healing from listening to music. How does this change how you feel about music? Have you ever experienced these effects in your own life?

3. Discuss the difference between music and worship. Biblically, prior to the fall in Genesis 3, do you think there was a difference between the two, or were they the same? How do we redeem the power of music to its original purpose?

4. Read 1 Samuel 16:1–23 together and discuss the link, if any, between verse 13 and verse 14. Then read Psalm 51:1–11. What was the context of this Psalm? Do you think that King David, being an eyewitness to what happened to King Saul once the Spirit had departed from him, could have been part of why he wrote, 'Cast me not away from your presence, and take not your Holy Spirit from me'? Have you ever lived without God's presence? What was that time like in your life?

5. Do you ever play worship in your home when you sense emotional, spiritual, or physical illness or pain? How could you intentionally do this during the next week? What triggers that you experience in your everyday life could become reminders or prompts to take a posture of worship?

Chapter Two: Worship Is a Weapon

1. Read Philippians 2:9–11. Reflect on, and discuss any moments in your own personal and corporate worship experiences where you have seen the name of Jesus change the spiritual atmosphere.

2. Have you ever felt that there has been a war for your personal worship? Have you ever heard the accusations of the enemy telling you that you are not worthy, clean or good enough to worship? You would not be alone if that has been your experience. Discuss your experiences with each other.

3. When you and your team lead the church in worship, is there space and room given for people to find victory in their lives? Do you have songs and moments that usher in this atmosphere of victory—lyrically and musically—and then songs that celebrate this victory?

4. Based on 2 Chronicles 20 and Jehoshaphat's warfare strategy, are there any battles in your own life that you need to approach differently? Share authentically around this. We grow together by sharing our hearts and lives with one another.

5. Read Isaiah 54:1–2 in a few different translations. Is there a room you are waiting to 'add to your house' that you are being invited to sing over? Ask the Holy Spirit to show you, and share your response.

Chapter Three: Worship Is Freedom

1. Spend a few minutes discussing what freedom looks like to you. Now talk about what freedom would look like in your church worship services.

2. Do you think you've ever fallen into the trap of 'yoking' yourself to what you do, rather than who you are? As you discuss this, reflect on the Dallas Willard quote, 'The most important thing in your life is not what you do, it's who you become.' Do you live like you believe this?

3. Read 2 Samuel 6:1–23. Given that David was the king, how significant and personally challenging do you find King David's freedom before God? Do you ever feel like you have had 'Michal's' in your life that have judged your freedom in worship? What have you done with that?

4. I shared my personal story of struggling to remember the last time I felt truly free. So now I ask you the same question—when was the last time you truly felt free? (Don't cheat, make sure your answer is outside of worship.)

5. Read 2 Corinthians 3:17. What could you do this week to live free? What could you do as a worship team to incorporate more moments of enjoying freedom as a church congregation?

Chapter Four: Worship Is Stillness

1. Be honest—how good are you at being still? Do you find it easy to be still on holidays or days off, or do you prefer to be moving?

2. The word *selah* means 'pause in silence'. Do you ever do this in your corporate worship? Do you ever lead your church in moments of pausing in silence?

3. Read Psalm 37:7. What was the key Hebrew word that we discussed from this passage? Have there been times in your life when you know you have been called to wait for God to move, but you rushed ahead? Can you think of any biblical examples of this?

4. In Luke 10:38–42, do you relate more readily with Mary or Martha? Why? Talk about this for a few minutes. Do you ever feel that you are so busy

serving God in worship ministry, that you neglect times to just sit at His feet? Be accountable to your friends and allow yourself to be real and tender in front of them. There is no condemnation in true covenant family.

5. Stillness in a world that never ceases is faith. It is an act of worship. How can you personally begin to incorporate times of stillness into your personal worship? What would this look like in your corporate setting? Discuss.

Chapter Five: Worship Is Pneuma

1. What kind of church environment did you grow up in? Was it an environment that embraced the Holy Spirit? What about your family of origin? How do you think this has affected the way you worship today? Do you think it has affected the way you lead worship?

2. What does the Hebrew word *ruah* mean, and how does it relate to the New Testament word, *pneuma*? Given the number of biblical references to the word *pneuma*, how important do you think the role of the Holy Spirit is to us as believers? What could it mean that the Holy Spirit is known as the 'wind' when it comes to our worship?

3. What do cessationists believe? What is your theology on the Holy Spirit? Do you know what your church's doctrine is on the role of the Holy Spirit? How does this affect the way you structure your worship services?

4. Read John 3:4–8. Now read verse eight again. What does this tell you about Spirit-led worship? Discuss this together.

5. Brainstorm together about how you could grow in following the wind of the Spirit in your worship. Are their areas of your skill that would need to grow? Would you need to spend more time doing this alone? Could you practice this together as a team? Could you come up with some simple four-chord progressions as a team that you could start to experiment with? Do you want to grow in this space, or does losing control scare you? Be honest with yourself and with each other.

Chapter Six: Worship Is Face to Face

1. Does it freak you out to think of making eye contact with Jesus? (It used to freak me out.) I came to realise that this was because I perceived Him to be angry with me. What do you think you would see in Jesus' eyes if you made eye contact with Him? Share what you journal or think in response to this.

2. Read 2 Corinthians 3:7–8, 18. Given the context of the worship life that we studied together of

Moses, what does this revelation open up to you in your personal worship life? What does it open up for your corporate worship experiences? Have you had any face-to-face encounters with God? Reflect, journal and share.

3. What things have you allowed to keep you at a distance from God? For me, it was insecurity, uncertainty, guilt and misconceptions about who God is. Ask the Holy Spirit if you believe any lies about yourself or about God that are affecting your intimacy with God. Share what is revealed to you. By bringing it into the light, you will remove its power.

4. Read Hebrews 4:16 in The Passion Translation. Journal a response to the truth you read. Share your response. Could you use this response as a springboard to play your instrument or write a melody? Try to stretch yourself to not use lyrics and to reflect the 'essence' of your response, remembering this is one of the biblical ways we worship, called *zamar*. These are great exercises to grow both your teams' practical and spiritual skills.

5. If we want to *become*, we have to *behold*. Take an honest examination of your personal worship practices. How much time do you spend *beholding*? Are you being changed by your worship practices? Because the more time you spend *beholding*, the more like Him you will *become*. Do you sing any songs in your corporate worship services that create lyrics and melody for people to *behold*? If not, consider and discuss doing so. When you offer these opportunities, you step into shepherding and leading your congregation at a whole new level because you are encouraging life transformation.

Chapter Seven: Worship Is Shoulder to Shoulder

1. Have you grown up in church like I have, or is church new for you? Reflect on what you love about the Church and what it brings to your life and then share around what you write.

2. Read Psalm 27 and notice how David writes about God's House and God's presence. Do you share David's love for the House of the Lord? Have you been hurt by the Church? Journal your response and then ask the Holy Spirit if this is affecting your love for His House. Share what you have journaled.

3. When you read the 1 Corinthians 12 metaphor of the Church as a body, what is the standout, light bulb moment for you? Why? Would you consider your church a well-functioning body? Reflect on why you have answered this way. Is it a 'you' thing

or a 'church' problem? Either answer is okay, just drill a little deeper and see what is at the heart of your response.

4. In Ephesians, Paul uses the Bride as a metaphor for the Church. Spend a moment reflecting on the preparation of a bride for her wedding. Then turn your thoughts to the emotion in the room when the bride enters the processional march. Contrast this with how you feel when the Church gathers for a service. Does it feel different or the same? Why is this? Does anything need to change?

5. What songs do you sing at church that tangibly bring a sense of unity? List as many of them as you can, and then see if you can identify a theme. You may have found the 'sound' of your house. To encourage healthy shoulder-to-shoulder worship, could you start to write or seek these kinds of songs in moments where the Body needs to be unified? I encourage you to do this with your whole song list. Write out every song you sing and then group them in themes. What themes work, and what themes are missing? As we have the privilege of leading shoulder-to-shoulder worship, these are important insights.

Chapter Eight: Worship Is Hide and Seek

1. Describe your prayer life in one sentence. Write it down and then share it with others. Don't be ashamed—be honest. It will help you grow in this important aspect of your worship.

2. Have you ever fallen into the trap of worshipping for appearances? It can be easy in platform ministry to worry more about how we look and sound during the service than on how we are ministering to God, can't it? Be honest before God and others. How are you going with the fear of man?

3. What does your secret place look like? Do you have a plan for how you read God's Word, pray, and spend time with Him? Is the platform the 1 percent of your worship life with Jesus or is it the total? Let me tell you, a lack of intimacy will eventually show itself up in public if we don't take care of it in private. I am constantly trying new things in my time with the Lord to keep it fresh. This could include a new Bible version, a new journal, a new instrumental soundtrack, or a new devotional method. I also love reading books on prayer so that I can keep growing in this space that I have often struggled in. Do what works for you, but write down and chat about your intentional growth in this area and offer to hold one another accountable.

4. Do you approach the Word of God for information or transformation? When we consider that we are told to approach God's Word like an animal to be sacrificed with its throat exposed (ouch), are you approaching His Word correctly? Reflect and share.

5. Are you walking in forgiveness? Go through the five-step process at the end of Chapter 8, and share what you experience. Some of the details may be too tender… that's okay. Just share how you felt before and after the process and whether or not you were surprised by what the Holy Spirit highlighted.

Chapter Nine: Worship Is a Mirror

1. Describe a season where you allowed walls to be put up in your heart that created distance between you and God. What was the root cause of this? Was it disappointment, anger or resentment? Journal this out and share.

2. Read Joshua 6:1–27. Reflect on, and discuss the role of worship and the worshipers in bringing down walls, not just for themselves, but also for the remainder of their families and people group. How could this be applied to what we do as lead worshipers?

3. Ray Hughes said, 'If pride turned angels into demons, guess what it will do to you and me.' Have you ever struggled with pride? How did it affect you? Reflecting on the story of Lucifer, how do we safeguard ourselves from falling into the same trap? What things do we need to have in our lives to keep us from going down prideful paths? Talk about how you could build a culture of humility within your team so that pride in an individual will deal with itself due to strong team culture.

4. Reflect on your personal worship times. Do they reflect your personal likes and dislikes lyrically, or do they reflect God's likes and dislikes? Now apply this same question to your corporate worship role.

5. In all honesty, how important is reflecting God outside of the church to you? Do you think that reflecting Him from a church stage is the fullness of your calling, or is there an overarching biblical call over your life outside the four walls of the church? Chat about how you can grow in your expressions of worship and reflections of God outside of the church.

Chapter Ten: Worship Is Both/and

1. 'Worship is not part of the Christian life, it is the Christian life' (Gerald Vann). Reflect honestly on this quote and be specific about how much of your life you have given Jesus reign over.

2. Reflecting on the secular/sacred divide, how open do you feel that the city, workplace, family and sphere in which God has placed you, are to your God story? Do you feel like you openly share about the difference Jesus has made in your life, or do you struggle with this? It can be so easy as the worship team to sing unashamedly about Him on Sunday but to fade into the background in our workplaces. Be honest with yourself and then with others, and ask for prayer to grow in boldness. We all need this! And most often, we need it when we step off the platform.

3. Do you have a vision for how the Church could affect the world in positive ways? Dream with God for a few minutes and think about what your city could look like if it was living according to God's Kingdom. Share your God dream with someone else and pray together for God's Kingdom to come on earth.

4. Do you feel more like 'Tiddalick', who keeps the living water hidden, or like Peter who became bold under the power of the Holy Spirit? Journal this before the Lord. Be honest with Him. Tell Him of your fears and ask Him for help—He wants to empower you to witness. Now talk with others about some things your team could do as outreach. How could you combine worship and evangelism? Remember, your identity is a child of God that has decided to become a disciple, and therefore, a disciple maker. You are called and mandated to make disciples. How can you do this with what is currently in your hands? Share your ideas.

5. Do you need to be freshly immersed in the Holy Spirit? This is not a once off thing. Biblically, we can be re-immersed over and over again. How hungry are you? Journal out your hearts desires to God. Why don't you spend some time as a team just worshiping and asking God to immerse you once again? And don't leave until you feel something shift. Friend, He always has more for you.

Finally, back to that opening reflection—let's play 'caption this' again. Complete this sentence: Worship is...

NOTES

Introduction: Worship Is Biblical

1. C. S. Lewis, quoted in *Truth Aflame: Theology for the Church in Renewal*, Larry D. Hart (Grand Rapids: Zondervan, 1999), 560.
2. Esau McCaulley, 'Worship', in *Lexham Theological Wordbook*, ed. D. Mangum, D. R. Brown, R. Klippenstein et al. (Bellingham, WA: Lexham Press, 2014), Logos Bible Software.
3. D. G. Peterson, 'Worship', in *New Dictionary of Biblical Theology*, ed. T. D. Alexander and B. S. Rosner (Downers Grove, IL: InterVarsity Press, 2000), 855–85, Logos Bible Software.
4. W. A. Elwell and B. J. Beitzel, 'Worship', in *Baker encyclopedia of the Bible*, vol. 2 (Grand Rapids, MI: Baker Book House, 1988), 2164.
5. Warren W. Wiersbe, *Real Worship* (Grand Rapids, MI, 2000), 20.
6. Acts 13:43, 50, 16:4, (English Standard Version).
7. Col. 2:18, (English Standard Version).
8. Rom. 12:1, (English Standard Version).
9. McCaulley, 'Worship', in Mangum, Brown, and Klippenstein et al., Lexham Theological Wordbook.

Chapter One: Worship Is Medicine

1. Carrie Barron, 'Music as Medicine, Songs as Solace', *Psychology Today*, March 14, 2014, https://www.psychologytoday.com/au/blog/the-creativity-cure/201403/music-medicine-songs-solace.
2. 'I Know Him So Well', Benny Anderson, Tim Rice, and Bjorn Ulvaeus, *Chess*, Hal Leonard, 1984.
3. R. R. Hutton, 'Korah (Person)', in *The Anchor Yale Bible Dictionary*, vol. 4, ed. D. N. Freedman (New York: Doubleday, 1992), 100.
4. Heather Craig, 'What are the Benefits of Music Therapy?' *Positive Psychology.com*, March 20, 2019, https://positivepsychology.com/music-therapy-benefits/.
5. Zoe Cormier, 'Music therapy: The power of music for health', *Science Focus*, October 9, 2018, https://www.sciencefocus.com/the-human-body/the-power-of-music-for-health/.
6. Isa. 10:27, (New King James Version).
7. 1 Sam. 10:1, (English Standard Version).
8. 'Who You Say I Am', Ben Fielding and Reuben Morgan, *There Is More*, Hillsong Music Australia, 2018.

Chapter Two: Worship Is a Weapon

1. Bill Johnson, *Hosting the Presence: Unveiling Heaven's Agenda* (Destiny Image, 2012), 34.
2. 'What a Beautiful Name', Ben Fielding and Brooke Ligertwood, *Let There Be Light*, Hillsong Music Australia, 2016.
3. Ibid.
4. Matt. 25:41, (English Standard Version).
5. Elwell and Beitzel, 'Lucifer', in *Baker encyclopedia of the Bible*, 1360.
6. Ibid.
7. 2 Chron. 17:3, (English Standard Version).
8. John Frederick, 'Praise and Thanksgiving', in *Lexham Theological Wordbook*, ed. D. Mangum, D. R. Brown, R. Klippenstein, and R. Hurst (Bellingham, WA: Lexham Press, 2014), Logos Bible Software.
9. Hebrews 12:2, (English Standard Version).
10. McCaulley, 'Worship', in Mangum, Brown, and Klippenstein et al., *Lexham Theological Wordbook*.
11. Matt. 17:20, (English Standard Version).
12. R. Jamieson, (n.d.), *A Commentary, Critical, Experimental, and Practical, on the Old and New Testaments: Joshua–Esther*, vol. 2 (London; Glasgow: William Collins, Sons, & Company), 543.
13. Theresa Dedmon, 'Co-Creating With God To Shape Our Story With Brian Simmons', *Create Talks with Theresa Dedmon*, April 15, 2020, https://www.theresadedmon.com/createtalks/co-creating-with-god-to-shape-our-story-with-brian-simmons.
14. James Swanson, *Dictionary of Biblical Languages with Semantic Domains: Hebrew (Old Testament)*, (Oak Harbor, WA: Logos Research Systems, Inc., 1997), Logos Bible Software.
15. Acts 16:20, (English Standard Version).
16. J. Strong, *The New Strong's Concise Dictionary of the Words in the Greek Testament and The Hebrew Bible*, vol. 1 (Bellingham, WA: Logos Bible Software, 2009), 61.
17. J. D. Barry, D. Mangum, D. R. Brown, M. S. Heiser, M. Custis, E. Ritzema, and D. Bomar et al., *Faithlife Study Bible* (Bellingham, WA: Lexham Press, 2012, 2016), Isaiah 54:1.

Chapter Three: Worship Is Freedom

1. A. W. Tozer, *Experiencing the Presence of God: Teachings from the Book of Hebrews* (Minnesota: Bethany House Publishers, 2010).
2. Rebekah Lyons, *You Are Free: Be Who You Already Are* (Michigan: Zondervan, 2017), 36.
3. C. L. Tyer, 'Yoke', in *The Anchor Yale Bible Dictionary*, vol. 6, ed. D. N. Freedman (New York: Doubleday, 1992), 1026.

4. Dallas Willard, quoted in *Soul Keeping: Caring for the Most Important Part of You*, John Ortberg (Grand Rapids: Zondervan, 2014).

5. Rom. 2:4, (English Standard Version).

6. D. M. Howard Jr., 'David (Person)', in *The Anchor Yale Bible Dictionary*, vol. 2, ed. D. N. Freedman (New York: Doubleday, 1992), 41.

7. Acts 13:22, (English Standard Version).

8. M. H. Woudstra, 'Ark of the Covenant', in *Baker encyclopedia of the Bible*, vol. 1 (Grand Rapids, MI: Baker Book House, 1988), 169.

9. M. P Matheney Jr., 'Ark of the Covenant', in *Holman Illustrated Bible Dictionary*, ed. C. Brand, C. Draper, A. England, S. Bond, E. R. Clendenen, and T. C. Butler (Nashville, TN: Holman Bible Publishers, 2003), 112.

10. 1 Sam. 7:2, (English Standard Version).

11. 1 Chron. 23:5, (English Standard Version).

12. J. R. Vannoy, *Cornerstone Biblical Commentary: 1-2 Samuel*, vol. 4 (Carol Stream, IL: Tyndale House Publishers, 2009), 300–301.

13. 2 Sam. 6:23, (English Standard Version).

14. 'Nothing Else', Cody Carnes, Hank Bentley, and Jessie Early, *Run To The Father*, Capitol CMG Paragon, 2019.

15. Dan McCollam, *Prophetic Company: the joyful journey toward building prophetic community* (Vacaville: Sound of the Nations, 2016), 41.

Chapter Four: Worship Is Stillness

1. Mark Buchanan, *The Rest of God* (Tennessee: Thomas Nelson, 2008).

2. James W. Goll, *The Lost Art of Practicing His Presence* (Shippensburg: Destiny Image Publishers, 2005).

3. Brian Webster and David R. Beach ed., *The Essential Bible Companion to the Psalms* (Michigan: Zondervan Academic, 2010), 16.

4. Barry et al., *Faithlife Study Bible*, Psalm 46.

5. Ibid.

6. Ibid.

7. McCaulley, 'Worship', in Mangum, Brown, and Klippenstein et al., *Lexham Theological Wordbook*.

8. J. D. Barry, D. Bomar, D. R. Brown, R. Klippenstein, D. Mangum, C. Sinclair Wolcott, W. Widder et al., ed., *The Lexham Bible Dictionary* (Bellingham, WA: Lexham Press, 2016), Logos Bible Software.

9. M. Mitchell, 'Selah', in *Holman Illustrated Bible Dictionary*, ed. C. Brand, C. Draper, A. England, S. Bond, E. R. Clendenen, and T. C. Butler (Nashville, TN: Holman Bible Publishers, 2003), 1459.

10. Dictionary.com, s.v. 'Stillness', accessed September 18, 2020, https://www.dictionary.com/browse/stillness?s=t.

11. Barry et al., *Faithlife Study Bible*, Psalm 37:7.

12. Wayne Muller, *Sabbath: Finding Rest, Renewal and Delight in Our Busy Lives* (New York: Random House, 2000).

13. Abraham Joshua Herschell, *Sabbath* (New York: Farra, Straus and Giroux, 2005).

14. Barry et al., *Faithlife Study Bible*, Luke 10:39.

15. James Swanson, *Dictionary of Biblical Languages with Semantic Domains: Greek (New Testament)*, (Oak Harbor, WA: Logos Research Systems, Inc., 1997), Logos Bible Software.

16. Lk. 10:41–42, (English Standard Version).

17. Dallas Willard, *The Spirit of the Discipline: Understanding How God Changes Lives* (New York: HarperCollins, 1988), 163.

18. 2 Cor. 12:9, (English Standard Version).

19. Peter Scazzero, *Emotionally Healthy Spirituality* (Nashville: Thomas Nelson, 2015), 151.

20. B. S. Easton, in T*he International Standard Bible Encyclopaedia*, vol. 1–5, ed. J. Orr, J. L. Nuelsen, E. Y. Mullins, and M. O. Evans (Chicago: The Howard-Severance Company, 1915), 2854.

Chapter Five: Worship Is Pneuma

1. Michka Assayas, *Bono: In Conversation with Michka Assayas* (New York: Riverhead Books, 2005).

2. Swanson, *Dictionary of Biblical Languages* (Old Testament).

3. 3 Job. 33:4; Ps. 33:6, (English Standard Version).

4. Ezek. 27:1–14, (English Standard Version).

5. 1 Sam. 10:5–6, (English Standard Version).

6. Barry et al., *Faithlife Study Bible*, John 3:8.

7. D. Seal, 'Pneuma', in *Faithlife Study Bible* (Bellingham, WA: Lexham Press, 2012, 2016), Logos Bible Software.

8. Dan McCollam, *A Prophetic Company* (Vacaville: Sound of the Nations, 2016), 30.

9. Ibid, 38.

10. Barry et al., *Faithlife Study Bible*, John 3:2.

11. E. A. Blum, in *The Bible Knowledge Commentary: An Exposition of the Scriptures*, vol. 2, ed. J. F. Walvoord and R. B. Zuck (Wheaton, IL: Victor Books, 1985), 281.

12. 'John 4:24 Word Wealth', in *New Spirit Filled Life Bible: NIV* (Nashville: Thomas Nelson, 2014).

13. G. M. Burge, 'John', in *Evangelical Commentary on the Bible*, vol. 3 (Grand Rapids, MI: Baker Book House, 1995), 853.

14. Barry et al., *Faithlife Study Bible*, Ephesians 6:17.

Chapter Six: Worship Is Face to Face

1. 'Ralph Waldo Emerson Quotes', BrainyQuote, accessed September 18, 2020, https://www.brainyquote.com/authors/ralph-waldo-emerson-quotes.
2. Gary Chapman, *The Five Love Languages: The Secret to Love that Lasts* (Chicago: Northfield Publishing, 2014).
3. Christian Jarrett, 'The Psychology of Eye Contact, Digested' Research Digest, November 28, 2016, https://digest.bps.org.uk/2016/11/28/the-psychology-of-eye-contact-digested/.
4. W. A. Elwell and B. J Beitzel, 'Moses', in *Baker Encyclopedia of the Bible*, vol. 2 (Grand Rapids, MI: Baker Book House, 1988), 1489.
5. Barry et al., *Faithlife Study Bible*, Exodus 33:11.
6. Swanson, *Dictionary of Biblical Languages (Old Testament)*.
7. 7 2 Cor. 3:1–18, (English Standard Version).
8. McCaulley, 'Worship', in Mangum, Brown, and Klippenstein et al., *Lexham Theological Wordbook. Wordbook*.
9. Swanson, *Dictionary of Biblical Languages (New Testament)*.
10. Barry et al., *Faithlife Study Bible*, 2 Corinthians 3:18.

Chapter Seven: Worship Is Shoulder to Shoulder

1. '20 Timeless Worship Quotes by A.W. Tozer', Renewing Worship, accessed September 18, 2020, https://www.renewingworshipnc.org/quotes-by-tozer/.
2. Jn. 5:19, (English Standard Version).
3. MP Dillon, LV Fortington, M Akram, B Erbas, and F Kohler, 'Geographic Variation of the Incidence Rate of Lower Limb Amputation in Australia from 2007-12', accessed September 18, 2020, https://www.limbs4life.org.au/australian-statistics.
4. Subedi Bishnu and George T Grossberg, 'Phantom limb pain: mechanisms and treatment approaches', *Pain research and treatment* vol. 2011 (2011): 864605. doi:10.1155/2011/864605.
5. 'Phantom Pain', Mayo Clinic Staff, Mayo Clinic, accessed September 18, 2020, https://www.mayoclinic.org/diseases-conditions/phantom-pain/symptoms-causes/syc-20376272.
6. MJE Neil, FRCA FFPMRCA, 'Pain after amputation', *BJA Education*, vol. 16, Issue 3, (March 2016), 107–112, https://doi.org/10.1093/bjaed/mkv028.
7. A. P. Ross, 'Psalms', in *The Bible Knowledge Commentary: An Exposition of the Scriptures*, vol. 1, ed. J. F. Walvoord and R. B. Zuck (Wheaton, IL: Victor Books, 1985), 888.
8. Exod. 30:22–32, (English Standard Version).
9. Ibid.
10. Barry et al., *Faithlife Study Bible*, 2 Corinthians 3:18.

11. Ezek. 47, (English Standard Version).
12. Barry et al., *Faithlife Study Bible*, Ezekiel 47:1–2.

Chapter Eight: Worship Is Hide and Seek

1. Henri Nouwen, *Making All Things New: An Invitation to a Spiritual Life* (New York: HarperCollins, 1981).
2. McCaulley, 'Worship', in Mangum, Brown, and Klippenstein et al., *Lexham Theological Wordbook*.
3. Swanson, *Dictionary of Biblical Languages (New Testament)*.
4. Timothy Keller, *Prayer: Experiencing Awe and Intimacy with God* (Great Britain: Hodder & Stoughton, 2014).
5. 'Aboriginal Religion—Part 1', Aboriginal Culture, accessed September 18, 2020, https://www.aboriginalculture.com.au/religion.html.
6. Harriet Sherwood, 'Non-believers turn to prayer in a crisis, poll finds', The Guardian, January 14, 2018, https://www.theguardian.com/world/2018/jan/14/half-of-non-believers-pray-says-poll.
7. 'Faith and Belief in Australia', McCrindle, accessed September 18, 2020, https://mccrindle.com.au/insights/blog/faith-belief-australia/.
8. Babynames.com, s.v. 'Stacey', 'Renee', accessed September 18, 2020, https://www.babynames.com.
9. Lk. 15:4, (English Standard Version).
10. Martin Luther, quoted in *Growing in Prayer: A Real–Life Guide to Talking with God*, Mike Bickle (Florida: Charisma House, 2014).
11. Eugene Peterson, quoted in *Seeking God's Face: Praying with the Bible Through the Year*, Philip F. Reinders (Michigan: Baker Publishing Groups, 2010), 10.
12. Swanson, *Dictionary of Biblical Languages (Old Testament)*.
13. Swanson, *Dictionary of Biblical Languages (New Testament)*.
14. 'Mobile Touches: dscout's inaugural study on humans and their tech', June 15, 2016, accessed 18 September, 2020, https://blog.dscout.com/hubfs/downloads/dscout_mobile_touches_study_2016.pdf.
15. University of Texas at Austin (UT Austin). 'The mere presence of your smartphone reduces brain power, study shows', *ScienceDaily*, (June 2017), accessed September 18, 2020, www.sciencedaily.com/releases/2017/06/170623133039.htm.
16. Ibid.
17. Robert M. Mulholland, *Shaped by the Word: The Power of Scripture in Spiritual Formation.* (Nashville: Upper Room Books, 1985), 40.
18. Swanson, *Dictionary of Biblical Languages (New Testament)*.
19. Barry et al., *Faithlife Study Bible*, 2 Corinthians 3:18.
20. J. K. Chamblin, 'Matthew', in *Evangelical Commentary on the Bible*, vol. 3 (Grand Rapids, MI: Baker Book House, 1995), 730.
21. Neil T. Anderson, *Who I Am In Christ: A Devotional* (Minnesota: Bethany House Publishers, 1993).

Chapter Nine: Worship Is a Mirror

1. A. W. Tozer, *A Disruptive Faith: Expect God to Interrupt Your Life* (Regal Publishing, 2011).
2. 'Jesus', Stacey Hilliar, *All I Need*, Garden City Christian Church, 2007.
3. D. K. Campbell, 'Joshua', in *The Bible Knowledge Commentary: An Exposition of the Scriptures*, vol. 1, ed. J. F. Walvoord and R. B. Zuck (Wheaton, IL: Victor Books, 1985), 340.
4. A. C. Bowling, 'Joshua', in *Evangelical Commentary on the Bible*, vol. 3 (Grand Rapids, MI: Baker Book House, 1995), 141.
5. Barry et al., *Faithlife Study Bible*, Joshua 6:5.
6. Campbell, 'Joshua', in Walvoord and Zuck, *The Bible Knowledge Commentary: An Exposition of the Scriptures*.
7. 1 Cor. 14:25, (English Standard Version).
8. Ps. 51:10, (English Standard Version).
9. Ray Hughes, 'From The Old to The New Testament', accessed 18 September, 2020, WorshipU, video, 16:47, https://www.worshipu.com/classes/heritage-of-worship/worship-through-the-ages/788.
10. 10 Ibid.
11. Swanson, *Dictionary of Biblical Languages (Old Testament)*.
12. Ibid.
13. Ibid.
14. Rev. 12:10, (English Standard Version).
15. Heb. 4:14–16, (English Standard Version).
16. Swanson, *Dictionary of Biblical Languages (Old Testament)*.
17. J. A. Witmer, 'Romans', in *The Bible Knowledge Commentary: An Exposition of the Scriptures*, vol. 2, ed. J. F. Walvoord and R. B. Zuck (Wheaton, IL: Victor Books, 1985), 487.

Chapter Ten: Worship Is Both/and

1. 'Gerald Vann Quotes', AZ Quotes, accessed September 18, 2020, https://www.azquotes.com/author/28957-Gerald_Vann.
2. 'The Historical Influence of the Sacred-Secular Divide', Institute for Faith, Work & Economics, October 17, 2016, https://tifwe.org/historical-influences-of-the-sacred-secular-divide/.
3. D. Kim, D. McCalman, and Dan Fisher, 'The Sacred/Secular Divide and the Christian Worldview', *J Bus Ethics* 109, 203–208 (2012), https://doi.org/10.1007/s10551-011-1119-z.
4. Bill Browne, 'Excessive Hours and Unpaid Overtime: 2019 Update', Centre for Future Work at the Australia Institute, November, 2019, https://www.tai.org.au/sites/default/files/GHOTD%202019%20Final_0.pdf.
5. Daniel I. Block, *For the Glory of God* (Baker Academic, Grand Rapids, MI; 2014).

6. John Mark Comer, *Garden City: Work, Rest, and the Art of Being Human* (Zondervan, Michigan, 2015), 94.

7. 'Faith and Belief in Australia: A national study on religion, spirituality and worldwide trends', McCrindle, May 2017, https://mccrindle.com.au/wp-content/uploads/2018/04/Faith-and-Belief-in-Australia-Report_McCrindle_2017.pdf.

8. D. J. Moo, 'Romans', in *New Bible Commentary: 21st Century Edition*, 4th ed., ed. D. A. Carson, R. T. France, J. A. Motyer, and Gordon J. Wenham, (Leicester, England; Downers Grove, IL: Inter-Varsity Press, 1994), 1115.

9. Barry et al., *Faithlife Study Bible*, Romans 12:1–21.

10. J. A. Witmer, 'Romans', in *The Bible Knowledge Commentary: An Exposition of the Scriptures*, vol. 2, ed. J. F. Walvoord and R. B. Zuck (Wheaton, IL: Victor Books, 1985), 487.

11. McCaulley, 'Worship', in Mangum, Brown, and Klippenstein et al., Lexham Theological Wordbook.

12. Ibid.

13. F. Brown, S. R. Driver, and C. A. Briggs, *Enhanced Brown-Driver-Briggs Hebrew and English Lexicon* (Oxford: Clarendon Press, 1977), 1036.

14. Block, *For the Glory of God*, 132.

15. Darlene Zschech, *Worship Changes Everything* (Grand Rapids, Michigan: Bethany House Publishers, 2015).

16. Block, *For the Glory of God*.

17. L. J. McGregor, 'Ezekiel', in *New Bible Commentary: 21st century edition*, 4th ed., ed. D. A. Carson, R. T. France, J. A. Motyer, and G. J. Wenham (Leicester, England; Downers Grove, IL: Inter-Varsity Press, 1994), 716.

18. Ezek. 47:1–12, (English Standard Version).

19. V. P Hamilton, 'Ezekiel', in *Evangelical Commentary on the Bible*, vol. 3 (Grand Rapids, MI: Baker Book House, 1995), 587–588.

20. 'Aboriginal Dreamtime' Artlandish, accessed September 18, 2020, https://www.aboriginal-art-australia.com/aboriginal-art-library/aboriginal-dreamtime/.

21. 'Tiddalick the Frog', Dreamtime, October 29, 2018, https://dreamtime.net.au/tiddalick-the-frog/.

22. Swanson, *Dictionary of Biblical Languages (New Testament)*.

ABOUT THE AUTHOR

Stacey and her husband Jai live in Melbourne with their four children, Noah, Cabe, River and Eden. They are on the Executive team at Neuma Church, which has multiple locations across Australia and one in Bangkok, Thailand.

Stacey is passionate about equipping and empowering individuals, churches, families and teams to grow in freedom, intimacy with Jesus, and build prophetic cultures with excellence in their love for the Church. Whether it is preaching, teaching, worship leading or writing, Stacey loves to represent the fullness of joy and freedom found in Jesus, and she's always up for a good laugh.

Stacey's favourite place is Paris, best enjoyed while eating a baguette, a good French drink and with the Eiffel Tower in the background.

A note from the author:

I would love to hear your thoughts on what you've read and what worship is to you. Please reach out on social media or at my website. I love connecting with like-minded people.

If you are interested in having me speak with your worship team or in your church, you can check out all the latest news below.

**STACEY HILLIAR
MINISTRIES**

Website: staceyhilliar.com
Instagram: @staceyhilliar
Facebook: facebook.com/stacey.hilliar